Further Praise for

DOUBLE ENTRY

"Stimulating. . . . Gleeson-White's book is not just fascinating history but a reminder that, as sociologist William Bruce Cameron wrote, 'Not everything that can be counted counts, and not everything that counts can be counted.'" —Drew DeSilver, *Seattle Times*

"A colorful description of the birth and development of double-entry bookkeeping. . . . A good read for the accountant and nonaccountant alike."

—Christopher Hemus,
Finance and Development magazine

"Through a fascinating and diverse historical cast of characters almost rivaling the cast of thousands in the *Ten Commandments* film, Gleeson-White weaves an intricate tale from Jericho, Mesopotamia, and the Renaissance, to the Industrial Revolution and the World Wars, to Wall Street and the modern global economy. She reminds us that accounting isn't just about numbers; it is also a form of storytelling that reveals the intentions and economic actions of the entity that is being accounted for. . . . Fascinating and engaging." —Daniel Osmer,
Associative Economics Café

"Elegantly written. . . . Charts the epic journey of the humble device that showed how to count the cost of everything, from the Doge's Palace to the acrobatics of John Maynard Keynes's *General Theory*."
—Nicholas Wapshott, author of *Keynes Hayek*

"The author makes ledgers and numbers come alive. . . . [This] spellbinding historical narrative . . . is sure to appeal to those in the accounting profession, business leaders, and history buffs, and will likely become required reading in business school curricula." —*Publishers Weekly*, starred review

"Compelling." —Timothy Spangler, *Los Angeles Review of Books*

"The book is the first primer to accounting history and its relevance to the modern world that I have ever seen. . . . The messages it contains are clear and unambiguous and all accountants, practicing or not, ought to note the tone of invocation for change. Jane Gleeson-White is to be congratulated for presenting us with clarity of appreciation of the issues facing mankind that accounting could do something about."—Alan Sangster, *Accounting History*

"Jane Gleeson-White has written a well-researched history. . . . Relevant and readable. . . . The author reminds us that history matters, even that of 'mundane professions,' because they 'increasingly run the capitalist world.' . . . The history of bookkeeping is an interesting one, and well told." —Luke Johnson, *Management Today*

"Spanning 500 years of history, *Double Entry* goes far beyond a mere historical account of accounting. It is a compelling argument that a Renaissance bookkeeping method should not be used as the primary measure of the financial health of multinational corporations and the wealth of nations." —Susan Meadows, *Pasatiempo*

"A stimulating approach that presents a compelling outline for further detailed review." —*Kirkus Reviews*

"Though a history of accounting might sound like dry reading, that is not the case in this narrative of the birth of double-entry bookkeeping in 15th-century Venice. Gleeson-White tells the story of double-entry bookkeeping to show the historical importance of keeping accounts, not only of cash and profits but also of resources."
—*Library Journal*

"Traces the story of double-entry bookkeeping from its first known origins, in the late thirteenth century, to its role in the twenty-first century global economy. . . . This book will appeal to history and business students."
—*Booklist*

"A lively and well detailed financial history survey recommended for business and general business holdings alike."
—*Midwest Book Review*

DOUBLE ENTRY

How the Merchants of Venice
Created Modern Finance

JANE GLEESON-WHITE

W. W. Norton & Company
New York · London

Manufacturing by Sterling Pierce
Book design by Peter Long
Production manager: Devon Zahn

Library of Congress Cataloging-in-Publication Data

Gleeson-White, Jane.
Double entry : how the merchants of Venice created modern finance / Jane Gleeson-White.
— 1st American ed.
p. cm.
Includes bibliographical references and index.
ISBN 978-0-393-08896-0 (hbk.)
1. Accounting—History. 2. Bookkeeping—History. 3. Bookkeeping—Italy—Venice–History. 4. Finance—Italy—Venice—History. 5. Finance—History. 6. Capitalism—History. I. Title.
HF5605.G54 2012
657.09–dc23

2012021100

ISBN 978-0-393-34659-6 pbk.

W. W. Norton & Company, Inc., 500 Fifth Avenue, New York, N.Y. 10110
www.wwnorton.com

W. W. Norton & Company Ltd., 15 Carlisle Street, London W1D 3BS

3 4 5 6 7 8 9 0

CONTENTS

For my father Michael Gleeson-White,
who told me tales of art and finance

And for Michael Hill, always

What advantages does the merchant derive from
Book-keeping by double-entry? It is amongst the
finest inventions of the human mind.

JOHANN WOLFGANG VON GOETHE, 1795

More than four hundred years ago, in the very first
book published on the subject, bookkeeping was
outlined in a form which still prevails around the
entire world.

A.C. LITTLETON, 1933

Historians often forget. Even the most mundane
professions have their history, and those mundane
professions increasingly run the capitalist world.

NORMAN DAVIES, 1996

BOBBY KENNEDY AND THE WEALTH OF NATIONS AND CORPORATIONS

O N 18 MARCH 1968, THREE MONTHS BEFORE AN assassin's bullet cut short his life, Senator Robert F. Kennedy made an impassioned speech at the University of Kansas. He spoke about the health of his nation, the economic powerhouse that is the United States of America, and the way we measure national wealth using figures such as the Gross National Product (GNP). Kennedy said:

> Too much and for too long, we seemed to
> have surrendered personal excellence and
> community values in the mere accumulation
> of material things. Our Gross National
> Product, now, is over $800 billion a year, but
> that Gross National Product—if we judge the
> United States of America by that—that Gross

National Product counts air pollution and
cigarette advertising, and ambulances to clear
our highways of carnage. It counts special
locks for our doors and the jails for the people
who break them. It counts the destruction
of the redwood and the loss of our natural
wonder in chaotic sprawl. It counts napalm
and counts nuclear warheads and armored cars
for the police to fight the riots in our cities.
It counts Whitman's rifle and Speck's knife,
and the television programs which glorify
violence in order to sell toys to our children.
Yet the Gross National Product does not allow
for the health of our children, the quality of
their education or the joy of their play. It does
not include the beauty of our poetry or the
strength of our marriages, the intelligence of
our public debate or the integrity of our public
officials. It measures neither our wit nor our
courage, neither our wisdom nor our learning,
neither our compassion nor our devotion to
our country, it measures everything, in short,
except that which makes life worthwhile.

Like many before and after him—including the GNP's
creator, Simon Kuznets—Senator Robert Kennedy
believed there was something profoundly wrong with
the way we calculate our national wealth and with the
numbers we produce to do so, such as the GNP and the

Gross Domestic Product (GDP). As Kennedy pointed out, these numbers generate alarming anomalies: in their parlance cigarette advertising is worth more than the health of a child. And yet today, forty years after Kennedy's call for their revision, these numbers continue to rule the policy decisions of governments, financial institutions, corporations and communities. These flawed numbers rule our lives.

How could we have got things so wrong?

And it is not just in our national accounting that things have gone so awry. From the notorious implosion in 2001 of the 1990s 'It Company', the energy giant Enron, to the near collapse of the global financial markets in 2008, we have witnessed a wave of spectacular cases of profoundly misleading, inscrutable and flawed corporate accounting.

On 27 February 2008, the 2007 annual accounts of the Royal Bank of Scotland were signed off. By asset size, the RBS was titanic. It was the biggest company in the world. The group's assets were larger than the GDP of many nations, including the United Kingdom's (which was £1.762 trillion versus the £1.9 trillion group assets of the RBS). As befits a massive financial institution entrusted with other people's money, the rhetoric of the company's 2007 annual report was responsible and measured: 'It is the Group's policy to maintain a strong capital base, to expand it as appropriate and to utilise it efficiently throughout its activities to optimise the return to shareholders while maintaining a prudent relationship between the capital base and the underlying risks of the business.'

A mere two months later, in April 2008, the so-called prudent bank was sinking, torpedoed by its exposure to toxic assets which left a £12 billion gaping hole in its balance sheet—a figure which soon stretched to £100 billion and counting. And yet nowhere is this multibillion-pound-sterling chasm evident in the group's accounts. Company accounts are supposed to be the tools by which corporate transparency is guaranteed for shareholders, the market and the public alike. And so shouldn't a massive shortfall of £12 billion be obvious in the RBS accounts? Or, as writer John Lanchester put it: 'By rights, by logic, and by everything that's holy, it should therefore be possible to see, somewhere in the accounts and the balance sheet, some clue to what went wrong—especially given that whatever went wrong must already have gone wrong, to hit the company so hard less than two months later.'

It was later revealed that the group had a much greater exposure to the sub-prime mortgage market than it had publicly admitted. Despite this apparent gross misrepresentation of the company's assets in February 2008, a spokesman for the RBS said: 'The Board was in possession of full information and the details provided to the market in all financial reporting reflected the Group's honestly held opinion at the time.'

This would become an all too familiar refrain over the coming months, as the behemoths of finance and banking toppled—Lehman Brothers, Lloyds-HBOS, AIG, Anglo Irish Bank, the Icelandic banks Glitnir and Landsbanki—all struck down by 'gigantic holes' that appeared, apparently out of nowhere, on the asset side of their balance sheets. And on their way down, these giants brought the international financial system to its knees. The costs of these collapses will be paid by tax-payers for decades.

Accounting generates annually published finan-cial statements that are meant to guarantee corporate transparency, thereby checking corporate behaviour and ensuring that markets function efficiently. These statements are the balance sheet, income statement, cash-flow statement and statement of retained earnings. But it turns out that these tools cannot be trusted to convey the true state of a business at all. And yet govern-ments, managers, policymakers and shareholders alike depend upon this information when making decisions that affect the lives of everyone.

How could we have got things so wrong?

Our world is governed by numbers generated by the accounts of nations and corporations. And yet these numbers are arbitrary, illusory. So how did we come to depend on these fallible beacons to direct our policies, institutions, economies, societies? Where did these false prophets, these numbers and accounts, come from?

This book is my attempt to answer these questions, and more. But these were not the questions I first asked myself when I set out to write it. Its evolution falls into three distinct stages. The original idea was born from a summer I spent in Venice as an intern at the Peggy Guggenheim Museum, when I was inducted into the mysteries and symbolic language of Italian Renaissance painting, and an economics degree I started the following year. Renaissance art and economics merged in my mind and I became curious about their relationship, about the wealth that made the art possible. I still have the yellow Post-it note which records my original intention for this book. It says: 'I'd like to celebrate the material origins of the Renaissance as we celebrate its fruits.' So, my first idea was to examine the neglected material foundations of the great Renaissance art we revere, which led me into the Dark Ages.

The Dark Ages turned out to be not so dark after all, or at least not in the emerging city-states of northern Italy. These cities—Pisa, Genoa, Florence and Venice—were swept up in a commercial explosion sparked at the end of the eleventh century by Pope Urban II's call in 1095 for Christian Europe to liberate Jerusalem from Islam, which prompted unprecedented numbers of people to march across Europe to the Holy Land and back again. Northern Italy became a major thoroughfare for these Christian warriors and business boomed. As trade flourished on ever greater scales, the northern Italians developed a new kind of record-keeping to cope with the growing complexity of their business dealings. It was perfected by the merchants of Venice and became known as bookkeeping *alla viniziana*: the

Venetian method. We know it today as double-entry bookkeeping.

The 'father' of double-entry bookkeeping was a Franciscan monk born near Florence in the 1440s. His name was Luca Pacioli. In 1494 he published the first printed treatise on Venetian bookkeeping. Very little has been written on him, but as I researched his life I became more and more fascinated. The monk was also a mathematician, the greatest mathematical encyclopaedist of the Renaissance. I learnt that he had been born in the same town and century as one of my favourite Renaissance painters, Piero della Francesca, who possibly taught Luca Pacioli mathematics. I then discovered that Pacioli had taught mathematics to my childhood hero, Leonardo da Vinci. And I began to understand that Pacioli's magnum opus, his mathematical encyclopaedia which contains his 27-page bookkeeping treatise, was published at a watershed in western history: the moment when mathematics was morphing from its medieval form into its incarnation as the lingua franca of science and the modern world. This, then, would be my book: the story of double-entry bookkeeping, Luca Pacioli and a revolution in mathematics—and in art.

It turned out that just as the wealth of Renaissance Italy was underpinned by a new method of bookkeeping, so the art of some of the greatest painters of the age was underpinned by mathematics—and Luca Pacioli was implicated in both revolutionary developments.

This book underwent a third transformation when I began to investigate the possibility that the system of national accounting first theorised by one of my economist heroes, John Maynard Keynes, might somehow be related to Pacioli's Venetian bookkeeping. I discovered that the very same double-entry bookkeeping principles used by the merchants of Venice had been used to construct the national accounts of the United States and Great Britain during the Great Depression and the Second World War.

And so this book became the story of double-entry bookkeeping itself, from its first known origins in late thirteenth-century Italy to its takeover of the twenty-first-century global economy.

The rise and metamorphosis of double-entry bookkeeping is one of history's best-kept secrets and most important untold tales. Why? First, because it arguably made possible the wealth and cultural efflorescence that was the Renaissance. Second, because it enabled capitalism to flourish, so changing the economies of the world forever. Third, because over several centuries it grew into a sophisticated system of numbers which in the twenty-first century governs the global economy. This medieval artefact is still in daily use around the world.

Finally, and most significantly, bookkeeping now has the potential to make or break the planet. Because accounting reduces everything to its monetary value, it has allowed us to value least that apparently free source of life itself: the planet. Through its logic we have let the planet go to ruin—and through its logic we now have a chance to avert that ruin. As *Guardian* journalist Jonathan Watts wrote in October 2010: 'So it has come to this. The global biodiversity crisis is so severe that brilliant scientists, political leaders, eco-warriors, and religious gurus can no longer save us from ourselves. The military are powerless. But there may be one last hope for life on earth: accountants.'

1

ACCOUNTING: OUR FIRST COMMUNICATIONS TECHNOLOGY

The origin of writing is no longer a mystery . . . Contrary to all expectations, writing has its roots deep in prehistory—going back to the ninth millennium BC. Nor would anyone have guessed that writing derived from counting.

DENISE SCHMANDT-BESSERAT, 2002

The role of merchants in medieval and early Renaissance society as instigators of economic, political and scientific innovation is seldom fully appreciated.

FRANK J. SWETZ, 1987

'ANODYNE PILLS FOR BREACHY . . . LAXATIVE PILLS for Ruth . . . syphilic Pills for Maria . . . oz 1 Antiphlogistie Anodyne Tincture . . . Bleeding Charlotte . . . oz 4 Powdered Rhubarb . . . Extracting one of your Negroes tooth . . . a Mercurial Purge for Cook

Jack . . .' This is a fragment found among the accounts of George Washington. As well as being a celebrated warrior and statesman, Washington was a successful entrepreneur who scrupulously recorded every business transaction of his farming, manufacturing and real estate empire with double-entry bookkeeping. Passed over for two hundred years in favour of his letters and diaries, Washington's extensive accounts speak volumes about his life and times—but only now are they being recognised as an invaluable part of Washington's story. This tale-telling quality of accounting records is contained in the word itself: 'account' relates not only to counting but also to storytelling. It encompasses both a 'statement of moneys, goods, or services received and expended, or other receipts and outgoings, with a calculation of the balance' and 'a narration, a report, a description'.

Our urge to account—to measure and record our wealth—is one of the oldest human impulses. We were accounting before we could use abstract numbers; we were accounting before we could write. In fact, it now appears that writing, one of the greatest human accomplishments, was invented by accountants. In 1969, the French archaeologist Denise Schmandt-Besserat began a research project that would take her more than two decades to complete and yield some staggering results. For 25 years she visited museums in the Near East, Europe and North America, examining thousands of artefacts—small pieces of clay that other

11

researchers had overlooked—which lay buried in their storerooms. Among figurines, pots and mud bricks, Schmandt-Besserat found fired clay tokens shaped as cones, spheres, ovoids and cylinders. Their purpose had eluded archaeologists and anthropologists for centuries.

As she grouped the tokens together, Schmandt-Besserat began to realise she had at her fingertips the remains of an ancient accounting system. The earliest tokens date back to around 7000 BC, when settled farming communities first appeared in Mesopotamia (now Iraq) and people began to keep track of their produce and exchanges. Schmandt-Besserat found that each shape represented a different thing: a cone was a small measure of grain, a sphere was a large measure of grain, and a cylinder was an animal. This simple token accounting method was our first symbol system created solely for communicating; it was our first visual code and the first technology invented for storing memory.

When cities emerged in around 3500 to 3100 BC— and with them bronze smithies, the potter's wheel, mass production kilns, merchants and large-scale trade—the tokens suddenly changed. A complex accounting system emerged. Now there were three hundred token shapes to record a wide range of goods, including bread, honey, textiles and metal; and the proto-accountants began to store their tokens in hollow clay balls, or 'envelopes', imprinted with the signature seals of the parties involved in the exchange. According to accounting historian

Richard Mattessich, the invention of clay tokens and envelopes—the sealed transfer of tokens between trade partners—was the origin of our modern accounting system. Interpreting Mesopotamian accounting in today's terms, Mattessich suggested that the total sum of tokens inside a clay envelope recorded an individual's assets, and therefore that putting a token into an envelope increased the owner's assets (or wealth) and was, by definition, the equivalent of a debit entry. Taking a token out of an envelope reduced the owner's assets and was thus the same as a credit entry. (In accounting, the terms 'debit' and 'credit' simply denote position in an account: debit means the left-hand side of an account; credit means the right-hand side. These terms and their use will be discussed in more detail in Chapter 4.)

The ancient accountants then began to press the tokens into the wet clay of the envelope, recording on its surface the number and sort of tokens it contained— and in the process took the first steps towards inventing writing. But the most significant advance occurred in around 3300 BC, when the record-keepers transformed the token-and-sealed-envelope system into something utterly new: they flattened out the clay balls and pressed the tokens into their flat surface—thus creating the world's first clay tablets.

The last step in the invention of writing was taken when the ancient traders realised they could simply draw the tokens' shapes on the tablets with a stylus, thus bypassing the tokens altogether; in other words, the 3-D tokens could be represented by 2-D symbols. And so spheres became circles, cones became triangles, ovoids became ovals and writing was invented. Writing remained the exclusive domain of account-keepers until about 2000 BC, when it began to be used in funerary rituals to commemorate the dead, and was subsequently taken up by a range of wordmongers, including law-makers, priests, historians and storytellers.

Apart from its role in the invention of writing, accounting is significant for human civilisation because it affects the way we see the world and shapes our beliefs. To take this early example, the invention of token accounting in Mesopotamia was important not only because it facilitated economic exchanges and generated writing, 'but because it encouraged people to see the world around them in terms of quantifiable outcomes'. For the first time we had tools which allowed us to count and measure—to quantify—the world around us and to record our findings.

All civilisations have recorded in one way or another their commercial transactions, and many of history's most illustrious artefacts relate to accounting. The Code of Hammurabi, a table of 282 Babylonian laws recorded around 1790 BC, includes several laws about account-ing. For example, number 104: 'If the merchant has given to the agent corn, wool, oil, or any sort of goods to traffic with, the agent shall write down the price and hand over to the merchant; the agent shall take a sealed memorandum of the price which he shall give to the merchant.'

Record-keeping and accountability reached new levels of sophistication in wealthy classical Greece and Rome, the first civilisations to use coinage. The Parthenon or Elgin Marbles from the fifth century BC contain accounting records, including the disbursements of the treasures of Athena, the ruling goddess of the city. The business dealings of all Athenian public officials were recorded, carved into stone and publicly displayed in Athens so its citizens could oversee the spending of state finances. Likewise, all Athenian citizens were required to keep regular accounts of their own financial affairs. If they failed to do so, they were severely punished by being forbidden to travel from the city, consecrate their property to a god, dedicate a sacred offering or make a will. Accountability and freedom of financial information were considered essential for running the world's first democracy.

The celebrated Roman orator Cicero launched his career in the law courts with prosecutions that rested on the evidence of accounting records, which were important legal documents in ancient Rome. The head of every Roman family was required to keep domestic accounts. In 77 BC, Cicero used the evidence of a client's well-kept ledger to argue in court for his good character and trustworthiness, saying, 'day-books last for a month, ledgers for ever . . . day-books embrace the memory of a moment, ledgers attest the good faith and conscientiousness which ensure a man's reputation for all time'.

The records of the most important account book of the Roman businessman (the *tabulae rationum*) were divided into two pages. The Roman naturalist Pliny the Elder was much taken with this division, which meant that two sides comprised the whole. In 70 AD he wrote: 'On one page all the disbursements are entered, on the other page all the receipts; both pages constitute a whole for each operation of every man.' Here, perhaps, are the rudiments of double-entry bookkeeping, which was to emerge in northern Italy some twelve hundred years later. Here too, in Pliny's appreciation of the fact that two pages make up the whole account—that the double constitutes the whole—lies some of the allure that double-entry bookkeeping has held for thinkers over the centuries as a metaphor for the dichotomies of human existence, or our tendency to divide the world into opposites: good and evil, life and death, body and soul, heaven and hell, labour and capital.

One of the most important documents of the very few which survive in Europe from the years between the fall of Rome in the fifth century and the Crusades is an accounting record called the *Capitulare de Villis*. Dating from 800 AD, it is a list of instructions for the management of royal estates initiated by Charlemagne, King of the Franks, or his son Louis. It instructs each estate manager or steward to 'make an annual statement of all our income, from the oxen which our plough-men keep, from the holdings which owe ploughing services, from the pigs, from the rents, judgement-fees and fines, from the fines for taking game in our forests without our permission', and so on. The list covers accounts for the entire enterprise of a feudal lord, from small details such as soaps and oils and the management of fish ponds to the business of battle: horses, smiths and shield makers. The annual income statement of the lord's estates was presented to him each Christmas, 'so that we may know the character and amount of our income from the various sources'.

Three hundred years after Charlemagne's accounting standards were formulated, feudal Europe was rocked to its foundations by an economic boom ignited by the Crusades—a series of mass movements ostensibly far from the concerns of commerce. In 1095, following an appeal from the Byzantine emperor for help against the Turks, Pope Urban II called all of Christendom to war against the infidel. The secular side effects of the Crusades catapulted Europe into a new epoch, opening it to the east as never before and reviving its stagnant economy. As historian A.C. Littleton put it: 'That Jerusalem was won and lost and won again mattered less to civilization, as it proved, than did the incidental results which formed no part of the original intention.'

These incidental results appeared first in the city-republics of northern Italy: Pisa, Venice, Florence and Genoa, trading centres which used their wealth or strategic position to free themselves from their feudal chains, from the rule of local aristocrats and the Church.

Pisa was the first to gain its freedom, granted

independence from its local lord by the Pope in 1081. Venice was next. In 1082, the Byzantine emperor's Golden Bull guaranteed Venetian merchants tax-free travel throughout the Byzantine empire west of Constantinople, in return for Venice's assistance with his battles against the Normans. The emperor's Golden Bull proved golden indeed: thirteen years after it was granted, the first Crusade reopened the eastern Mediterranean— and the merchants of Venice found themselves kings of a lucrative trade empire which spread to Greenland in the north and east to Peking.

One of the new breed of Italian merchant travellers was the legendary Venetian Marco Polo (c. 1254–1324), who in 1271 travelled with his father and uncle across the Gobi Desert to the court of the Mongol emperor Kublai Khan. His *Book of Various Experiences* was one of the few first-hand European accounts of eastern Asia before the seventeenth century and was used as a guidebook by explorers such as Christopher Columbus.

Another widely travelled Italian merchant of the thirteenth century was Leonardo da Pisa, better known today as Fibonacci (c. 1170–1240), who grew up on the coast of Barbary, now Algeria, where his father worked at the Pisan customs house. The young Fibonacci spent his days in the local bazaars, where he was captivated by the extraordinary system of writing numbers the Arab merchants used to conduct their business. He later wrote: 'There, following my introduction, as a consequence of marvelous instruction in the art, to the nine digits of the Hindus, the knowledge of the art very much appealed to me before all others.' The numerals used by the Arabs in bazaars across the Mediterranean—in Egypt, Syria, Greece, Provence—could be applied to computations Fibonacci had never seen before, such as addition, subtraction and multiplication. This simple Arabic arithmetic we all use today was mostly unknown in Europe at the time. Instead, those Europeans who could write used Roman numerals to record numbers and a counting board, or abacus, to add and subtract. At its simplest, this was a sand-covered board (*abax* in the Greek, hence *abacus* in Latin) with pebbles (*calces* in Latin, hence 'calculation') used for counting.

The Arab merchants had learnt their number system in India by the ninth century and had been using it for centuries to calculate interest, convert currencies and solve other problems of trade. Fibonacci brought these Hindu–Arabic numerals (also known as Arabic numerals) to Italy where he wrote several books about them in Latin and became a celebrated mathematician. The most famous of his books, the 1202 *Liber abaci* ('Book of Calculation'), begins: 'These are the nine figures of the Indians: 9 8 7 6 5 4 3 2 1. With these nine figures and with this sign 0 which in Arabic is called zephirum, any number can be written, as will be demonstrated.' In the *Liber abaci* Fibonacci explained the new numbers, giving examples of the practical problems they could solve and the theoretical problems they posed, such as the growth of a rabbit population, which generates the famous 'Fibonacci numbers'. This is a sequence starting with 0 and 1 in which each subsequent number is the sum of the first two (0, 1, 1, 2, 3, 5, 8, 13, 21, et cetera) and which is found in the growth patterns of most living things. The *Liber abaci* became the most influential book on Hindu–Arabic numerals and arithmetic in Europe, although it would take three hundred years for the mathematical system it promoted to become widely used there.

The earliest known surviving Italian account is a fragment from the ledger of a Florentine bank dated 1211, nine years after the appearance of Fibonacci's *Liber abaci*. It records the debtors and creditors of a customer from Bologna and shows in embryo the features of a modern ledger, except that it uses Roman numerals to record money amounts which would have been calculated with an abacus.

Most accounting historians agree that the first surviving accounts kept in double entry date to around 1300: the accounts of the Florentine merchants Rinieri Fini & Brothers (1296–1305) and those of Giovanni Farolfi & Co. (1299–1300). The Farolfi ledger displays the six essential features of double-entry bookkeeping as outlined by accounting historian G.A. Lee: first, the idea of a proprietor or business partnership as an accounting entity whose books record its financial relationships with others. Second, its entries are made in a single monetary unit so they can be added together. Third, it relates the following oppositions: increases and decreases in physical holdings of cash or goods; increases and decreases in debts by or to other individuals or entities; and increases and decreases in the business's own assets and liabilities. Fourth, owner's equity is shown as the sum of assets and liabilities. Fifth, profit is understood to be the net increase in the owner's equity (and loss the net decrease). Sixth, the profit or loss is measured over a clearly defined accounting period.

The appearance of these first double-entry accounts in Italy so soon after the arrival of Hindu–Arabic numerals is provocative, and provides an alternative to the commonly given explanation for the emergence of double-entry bookkeeping in Europe around 1300—which is that it was the result of a phenomenal expansion in commercial activity, particularly in thirteenth-century Florence. This usual explanation is persuasive: that with their unprecedented concentrations of capital raised through their unique system of commercial partnerships built on family alliances, their many partners who each required their individual capital contribution and responsibilities to be recorded, and their vast credit networks which spanned Europe, the successful merchant bankers of Florence would have been forced to devise systematic new methods of bookkeeping—no longer would a single merchant's memory or a few diary pages suffice. And so, the story goes, the Florentine record-keepers developed a style of account-keeping which allowed them to classify, record and cross-check their accounts—and, most importantly, to calculate their profits, which allowed them to see not just what they owned but also how well their business was doing. This new form of business recording was double-entry bookkeeping.

It is also possible, however, given the timing, that the new mathematics and double-entry bookkeeping evolved together in Asia as part of a coherent commercial system developed by the Hindus or Arabs, or both. Research into the possible Islamic or Hindu origins of double-entry bookkeeping has found suggestive but no conclusive evidence. Some researchers have traced the new bookkeeping to Fibonacci's *Liber abaci* and to the Islamic universities of Muslim Spain. Others argue that accounting practices in the early Islamic State (founded in 622) were similar to those later used in northern Italy and may have been their source.

But it is also possible that Indian merchants originally developed the art. In the eighteenth century the British traveller Alexander Hamilton wrote: 'We would remark that the *Banias* [traders] of India have been, from time immemorial, in possession of the method of book-keeping by double-entry' and noted that in the Middle Ages Venice was 'the emporium of Indian commerce'—implying that Venice was the gateway through which double entry reached Italy from India. Although there is very little surviving documentary evidence of ancient Indian commercial practice, it seems that this Indian double-entry system—known there as *bahi-khata*—was used by its merchants for possibly thousands of years.

The new style of bookkeeping was just one of several technical innovations that appeared in Europe in the thirteenth and fourteenth centuries which emphasised precision, mathematics and the quantification of physical phenomena. Among these inventions were spectacles to correct eyesight, written marine charts for navigation, the first frescoes painted using artificial perspective, and the first European clocks. A town clock soon became de rigueur in wealthy European cities and these civic clocks began to be used to regulate daily life. In April 1335, Philip VI of France gave the mayor and aldermen of Amiens the power to set, and control by a bell, the time the city's workers went to work in the morning, ate their lunch in the middle of the day, and finished work in the afternoon. In 1370 Charles V attempted to standardise time throughout Paris by decreeing that all the city's clocks be set according to his palace clock on the Île de la Cité.

This enthusiasm for measuring was fuelled by a burgeoning new class—the merchants. The increasing influence of merchants in medieval and early Renaissance Europe gave birth to a civilisation in which for the first time people could satisfy their needs 'only by buying the services of and granting privileges to those who lived by counting'. One of these new counting men was Francesco Datini, a merchant from Prato, near Florence, a cloth manufacturer and dealer in armour, wool, wheat and slaves. On his death in 1410—without legitimate children—Datini bequeathed to Prato not only his fortune of 70,000 gold florins but also 500 account books, 300 deeds of partnership, 400 insurance policies, bills of exchange, cheques and some 150,000 letters. At the height of his business life, Datini exchanged 10,000 letters a year—with his wife (who remained in Prato while he lived and worked mostly in Florence); his friends; his trading houses in France, Italy, Spain and Majorca; and his agents throughout the Mediterranean and across Europe from Bristol to the Black Sea. Two themes preoccupied Datini's restless mind and infuse his many letters: religion and business. And he invoked both in the opening dedication of every ledger he used: 'In the name of God and of profit'. Like Shakespeare's merchant of Venice, Datini worried constantly—about his merchandise, about the safety of the ships that carried his wares, about the health of the sailors, the threat of pirates, the ravages of the plague. Towards the end of his long, healthy and prosperous life, Datini wrote to his wife: 'Destiny has ordained that from the day of my birth I should never know a whole happy day.'

Datini's meticulously kept account books span almost fifty years and clearly show the transition from single- to double-entry bookkeeping. His surviving ledgers from 1367 to 1372 do not use the double-entry system, while those from 1386 onwards do. Datini was innovative not just in his early adoption of the new style of bookkeeping; when in 1398 he and a partner opened a bank in Florence, they accepted a new form of payment only just coming into use in Europe: cheques. Like many business practices new to medieval Europe, the cheque had long been used by Arab merchants, who gave us the English word 'cheque'. As early as the ninth century a Muslim merchant could cash a cheque in China drawn on his bank in Baghdad.

Datini also dealt in bills of exchange, which were notes for the exchange at a future date of florins for one of the many different currencies circulating in Europe at the time, when every city minted its own coins. These bills first appeared in Europe in the twelfth century and became a powerful new financing tool. In Datini's day, charging interest on a loan at a fixed rate was outlawed by the Church, which deemed it usurious. (Demanding interest on loans was not permitted anywhere in Europe until 1545, when Henry VIII legalised it in England.) Bills of exchange became popular because, while they attracted a profit, they eluded the Church's ban on usury. Paradoxically, their popularity rested on their unreliability. Bills of exchange were effectively gambles on exchange-rate variations, and the chance of making a profit from them was so uncertain, so precarious, that the Church did not recognise their profits as interest and therefore allowed their use. Nevertheless, banking generally, and bills of exchange in particular, were still regarded with suspicion. When Datini opened his bank a friend wrote to him: 'Divers men have said to me, Francesco di Marco [Datini] will lose his repute as the greatest merchant in Florence, by becoming a

money-changer; for there is not one of them who prac-
tises no usury in his contracts. I became your advocate,
saying you mean still to be a merchant as before, and if
you keep a bank, it is not to practise usury.'

Datini was one of the new breed of Italian international merchant bankers who in the fourteenth century
created vast trading empires and networks of credit from
London to Constantinople. In the next century these
Italian international merchant bankers, most notably
the Medici of Florence, would use their immense wealth
to commission works of architecture, art and scholarship—and effectively finance the Renaissance. Datini
stood on the threshold of this new age, a man ahead
of his time. For in Datini's day the restrictive, secretive
guild system of medieval Europe still ruled trade and
commerce. Early double-entry accounts such as Datini's
were kept not with the new Hindu–Arabic numerals but
in the old, inoperable Roman numerals; only by the end
of the fifteenth century did Hindu–Arabic numerals
begin to appear in accounting records.

Despite their greater efficiency and versatility, the
new numerals took three hundred years to be accepted
in Italy. Their use was discouraged and often outlawed
by the guilds and other power players such as the Church
who believed that Roman numerals were superior and
tamper-proof, and the scandalous new eastern numerals
easy to alter and falsify. In 1299 the Florentine Arte di
Cambio (Guild of Money Changers) banned the use of
Hindu–Arabic numbers. The Medici bank did not use

Hindu–Arabic numerals exclusively until about 1500, and the last Italian book of arithmetic in Roman numerals was published as late as 1514. Elsewhere in Europe the adoption of Hindu–Arabic numerals was even slower: in 1520 the German municipality of Freiburg refused to accept accounts as legal proof of debt unless they were made in Roman numerals or written out in words; and Roman numerals were still used in Scotland in the seventeenth century.

However, the use of Hindu–Arabic numerals *was* advocated by the man who in 1494 codified the state-of-the-art bookkeeping practices of Venice. By the 1430s the merchants of Venice had perfected a system of double-entry account-keeping in two columns which became known as bookkeeping *el modo de vinegia* or *alla viniziana*: the Venetian method. It is this Venetian method that, through its extraordinary resilience and mutability, has come down to us today, transformed over several centuries from a rudimentary business tool into an efficient calculating machine.

The man responsible for its codification and preservation—the author of the world's first printed bookkeeping treatise—is Luca Bartolomeo de Pacioli, Renaissance mathematician, monk, magician, constant companion of Leonardo da Vinci. As the origin of all subsequent bookkeeping treatises throughout Europe, Luca Pacioli's bookkeeping tract is not only the source of modern accounting but also ensured the medieval Venetian method itself survived into our times. And so accountants have named Luca Pacioli the 'father of accounting'—and any story of double entry must pay him special attention. It is worth examining in some detail not only Pacioli's life but also his times, because in his century Italy was shaken by a renaissance in mathematics and a communications revolution which both bore directly on the staying power of double entry itself.

2

MERCHANTS AND MATHEMATICS

Pacioli's achievements reflect the coming together of
several key factors which together altered the world:
printing, the popularisation of Hindu–Arabic numerals
and the rise of mercantile capitalism.

FRANK J. SWETZ

In our change-loving Italy, where nothing stands
firm and where no ancient dynasty exists, a servant
can easily become a king.

ENEA SILVIO PICCOLOMINI (LATER POPE PIUS II), 1458

LUCA PACIOLI'S DOUBLE-ENTRY BOOKKEEPING TREA-
tise *Particularis de computis et scripturis* ('Particulars
of Reckonings and Writings') was published in his mathematical encyclopaedia in Venice in 1494, forty years
after the invention of movable type in Europe and the
fall of Constantinople to the Ottoman Turks. It appeared
in the same decade that Columbus sighted America and
Vasco da Gama discovered a sea route to India, at a
time when mathematics was taught as astrology in the

universities of Europe and witches were burnt at the stake. And yet five hundred years later his bookkeeping treatise remains the foundation of modern accounting and its system is still in use throughout the world. This is extraordinary.

There is no record of Luca Pacioli's childhood. All we know about his early life is the place of his birth—the small market town of Sansepolcro, now in Tuscany— and the year: 1446 or 1447. Five years earlier the town had been sold to Florence by its ally, the Pope, after they had defeated their common enemy—Milan—at the famous Battle of Anghiari. Machiavelli tells the tale: 'As the Pope, notwithstanding the victory at Anghiari, lacked money for [his] various enterprises, he sold the castle of Borgo San Sepolcro to the Florentines for the sum of twenty-five thousand ducats.' This is significant because it meant that Sansepolcro came under the sway of Florence, then the centre of the Italian avant-garde: Humanism (an intellectual movement focused on the study of the pagan literature of classical Greece and Rome, especially the work of Cicero), and the revolutionary new art of perspective painting.

SANSEPOLCRO
~

Sansepolcro lies at the geographic heart of Italy, on the fertile plain of the upper Tiber Valley almost directly north of Rome and about eighty kilometres southeast of

Florence. Its name comes from a legend about the tomb of Christ (which is known as the Holy Sepulchre or, in Italian, the *Santo Sepolcro*). According to the legend, at the close of the tenth century two Christian pilgrims, Egidio and Arcano, were travelling home from Jerusalem carrying fragments of the Holy Sepulchre. On their way north through the Tiber Valley from Rome the pilgrims paused to rest for the night. As they slept, they were told in a dream to stop where they were camped and build a chapel to house the sacred relics they had brought with them from the Holy Land. They obeyed the voice and built a chapel dedicated to the Santo Sepolcro. It soon became an important site for Christian pilgrims, and over the years a town grew up around it called Borgo San Sepolcro. By 1012 the original chapel had been replaced by an abbey which still stands today in the city known as Sansepolcro.

In the twenty-first century the old walled centre of Sansepolcro is almost as it was in Pacioli's day. Narrow stone-paved streets cut a grid across the town and open into a luminous central piazza, where several of the faded terracotta buildings date back to the eleventh century. Beyond the walls of the old city, modern Sansepolcro reaches up into the foothills of the Apennines and across the verdant Tiber Valley.

Pacioli is still remembered in the town of his birth. There is a street dedicated to him, via Luca Pacioli. In the Piazza Fra Luca Pacioli by the northern wall of the old town near the church of San Francesco, a white marble statue of the mathematician dressed in monk's robes and holding an open book commemorates the five hundredth anniversary of the publication of his greatest work, the encyclopaedia *Summa de arithmetica, geometria, proportione et proportionalità* ('Everything about Arithmetic, Geometry, Proportion and Proportionality'). And a plaque erected in 1878 on a building opposite the Civic Museum honours both his achievements in algebra, geometry and double-entry bookkeeping, and his friendships with two giants of the Renaissance, Leon Battista Alberti and Leonardo da Vinci.

But Sansepolcro is more famous today as the birthplace of another of its great fifteenth-century sons, Pacioli's older contemporary, the painter and mathematician Piero della Francesca (c. 1412–92). Piero's *Resurrection*—his fresco of Christ rising from his sepulchre painted around 1463—has become the emblem of Sansepolcro and the focus of its tourist industry. In an extraordinary twist of fate, the town even owes its survival during the Second World War to this painting. In 1944 the British 8th Army, under the charge of battery commander Anthony Clarke, was positioned around Sansepolcro, ready to destroy it. Clarke's field-gun battery had begun firing when suddenly he remembered why the name 'Sansepolcro' was so familiar to him. Several years earlier he had read an essay by Aldous Huxley called 'The Best Picture' (1925), which described a sublime painting in a small Tuscan town, the very town he was about to decimate. In his essay Huxley describes Sansepolcro as a 'little town surrounded by walls, set in a broad flat valley between hills; some fine Renaissance palaces with pretty balconies of wrought iron; a not very interesting church, and finally, the best picture in the world'—Piero's *Resurrection*, his painting of Christ emerging from his sepulchre, one draped leg resting firmly on its rim, his gaze aimed squarely at the viewer, his muscled chest gashed and bleeding, and his four guards lost in sleep. Huxley wrote: 'We need no imagination to help us figure forth its beauty; it stands there before us in entire and actual splendour, the greatest picture in the world.' Remembering Huxley's words, Clarke immediately ordered the bombardment to stop. The town and Piero's *Resurrection* were saved. Sansepolcro later immortalised its saviour by naming a street in Clarke's honour, the via A. Clarke.

Fittingly for the birthplace of the 'father of accounting', the story of Sansepolcro from its origins to the decade of Pacioli's birth is one of sale and purchase. It was first governed by the Church, but at the end of the fourteenth century it was sold by the Pope's nephew to the rulers of Rimini (the Malatesta family) on the Adriatic coast. Sansepolcro flourished under the Malatesta and became a busy market town, trading in the bounty of the Tiber Valley: timber, woollens, silks, hides, and woad, a blue dye for which it became famous.

Malatesta rule came to an end with the sort of transaction that would in the next century trigger the Reformation: in 1430, two illegitimate Malatesta sons gave the town to the Pope in exchange for a papal letter which legitimised their births. For the next ten years the town was fought over by the nearby Florentines allied with the new Pope, Eugenius IV, against their common enemy, Milan. The conflict ended in 1440 with the Battle of Anghiari and the delivery of Sansepolcro into Florentine hands. Thanks to its new rulers, by the late 1440s the town had become a rich trading centre with a population of about 4300 (nearby Urbino, a major city, had a population of no more than 6000 at the height of its power), and spent its newfound wealth on building palazzos and commissioning works of art, mostly from Piero della Francesca.

The first we know of Luca Pacioli is that as a young boy he was taken into the family of the local merchant Folco de' Belfolci, probably as an apprentice, where he would have been introduced to mathematics. To understand the full force of Luca Pacioli's contribution to the history of accounting, we must understand the profound transformation that occurred in Italian mathematics after the fall of Constantinople to the Turks in 1453.

A STORY OF MATHEMATICS

~

In the fifteenth century, Italian mathematics absorbed two significant new elements: Hindu–Arabic arithmetic; and ancient Greek mathematics, which was rediscovered first through secondary Arabic sources and later, after the fall of Constantinople, through the Greek originals. The same century also saw the merging of two streams of mathematics which had been split since the sixth century BC: the philosophical-speculative mathematics of Pythagoras and his successors, and the commercial arithmetic used by merchants. The mix would prove epoch-changing. It spurred the gradual rise of mathematics to its eventual usurpation of Latin as the lingua franca of Europe and ushered in a new era: the Age of Science.

Mathematics springs from two ancient sources, born from the dark arts of Egyptian priests and the commercial activities of early merchants. The title of one of the first known works on mathematics—the Egyptian papyrus *Directions for Knowing All Dark Things* (c. 2000 BC)—clearly conveys its connection to esoteric knowledge and its perceived access to the powers of darkness. The papyrus deals with fractions, arithmetic and geometry, and was intended for priests. A warning attributed to Augustine some 2400 years later reveals the abiding association of mathematics with magic and the dark arts: 'The good Christian should beware of mathematics and all those who make empty prophecies. The danger already exists that mathematicians have made a covenant with the devil to darken the spirit and confine man in the bonds of Hell.' As we shall see, the association of maths and magic is one that would be maintained by Luca Pacioli and continues to this day.

According to the ancient Greek historian Herodotus, geometry—which would become the sacred, speculative branch of mathematics—originated in Egypt and was associated with the land surveying required for the annual flooding of the Nile, hence 'geo-metry', from the Greek for 'earth' and 'measure'. Commercial arithmetic, on the other hand, was developed by the Phoenicians, the great merchants of the early Mediterranean. But ironically, it was the son of a Phoenician merchant who 'purified' mathematics by lifting it above the mundane needs of merchants to the realm of metaphysics: Pythagoras (c. 569–500 BC). Pythagoras and his followers boasted that in mathematics they sought pure knowledge and not the wealth its application might bring. And so from Pythagoras onwards mathematics was split into two broad streams: the calculations used by merchants in their daily business transactions, and the numbers used by philosophers to express the secret harmonies of the universe.

The Pythagoreans divided mathematics into four subjects—arithmetic (or numbers absolute), music (numbers applied), geometry (magnitudes at rest), and astronomy (magnitudes in motion)—with geometry as the cornerstone of all education. These four subjects were known as the 'quadrivium' and became the foundation of a liberal education in Europe until the Renaissance. The Pythagoreans believed the numerical relationships they found in nature (such as *pi*) could explain the order and harmony of the universe, that numbers in some way constitute the universe, and are not just the tools used to measure and describe it as we generally consider them to be today.

The idea that the secrets of the universe are found in numbers influenced generations of ancient Greek philosophers, including Plato (c. 428–348 BC), who wrote over the gateway to his academy: 'Let none ignorant of geometry enter my door.' Plato also believed that numbers were the language of the created world, as he wrote in one of his least read dialogues, the *Timaeus*: 'God made the sun so that animals could learn arithmetic— without the succession of days and nights, one supposes, we should not have thought of numbers. The sight of day and night, months and years, has created knowledge of number and given us the conception of time, and hence came philosophy.' Plato's belief in the metaphysical properties of numbers profoundly shaped western philosophy, theology and mathematics. Even Archimedes (c. 287–212 BC)—the greatest mathematician of the ancient world, famous for applying mathematics to the problems of everyday life in his inventions such as the siege engine and screw pump—thought it 'undesirable for a philosopher to seek to apply the results of science to any practical use'.

The collected knowledge of ancient Greek mathematics, including the work of Pythagoras, was compiled by the Greek mathematician Euclid in around 300 BC in his book the *Elements*, which became a standard textbook in ancient Greece and the basis of education in Europe until the twentieth century. Euclid's *Elements* was the most successful textbook ever written and, until it fell out of use in the 1900s, the second best-selling book of all time after the Bible.

Following the fall of Rome, Greek mathematics survived in Europe in fragmented and reduced form in the cathedral and monastery schools set up by Charlemagne in the eighth century, which taught the Pythagorean mathematical quadrivium alongside the 'trivium' of grammar, logic and rhetoric. The mathematics taught, however, was basic: enough arithmetic to keep accounts, music for church services, geometry for land surveying, and astrology to calculate the dates of Christian feasts and fasts; it used Roman numerals, the abacus, and Latin translations of Greek mathematics (especially Euclid) by the Roman scholar Boethius (c. 480–524). The mathematics known to the educated of medieval Europe was rudimentary, held in check by the Christian Church.

But in the Arab world it blossomed. By 1200, the Arabs were the most sophisticated mathematicians of the Mediterranean. They adopted and developed Hindu numerals, algebra and arithmetic, including 'the Rule of Three'. This is a simple method of finding an unknown from three known interrelated items which was used to solve most problems of commercial arithmetic—for example, 'There is a fish that weighs 60 pounds, the head weighs ⅗ of the body and the tail weighs ⅓ of the head. I ask what the body weighs'.

One of the greatest Arabic mathematicians was Muhammad ibn Musa al-Khwarizmi of Baghdad. His

Book of Addition and Subtraction According to the Hindu Calculation, written in the ninth century, is the earliest known work on Hindu mathematics and its twelfth-century translation into Latin became one of the key sources on the subject in Europe. Al-Khwarizmi also wrote a treatise on algebra, *Kitab al-jabr wa'l-muqabala* ('The Book of Restoring and Balancing'), which gave us the English word 'algebra' (from the 'al-jabr' of the title). Al-Khwarizmi was the first to regard algebra as a branch of mathematics of equal importance to the traditionally more glamorous geometry, and he established algebraic analysis as a discipline in its own right.

Arab mathematics and its Greek sources were first introduced to western Europe through Muslim Spain, where two important translations were made in the twelfth century. The first, of Euclid's *Elements*, was by the intrepid English monk Adelard of Bath, who travelled to Spain in search of Arab learning and discovered their work on Euclid at a famous Moorish college in Cordova. The other great mathematical translation of the twelfth century was of al-Khwarizmi's work, transcribed into Latin by Robert of Chester, another itinerant Englishman who travelled to Spain seeking its cutting-edge Islamic scholarship. Robert's translation introduced European scholars to Hindu–Arabic mathematics. But, as we have seen, Europeans were slow to adopt the new mathematics from the east. Only with the appearance in 1202 of Fibonacci's *Liber abaci* (originally titled *Algebra et almuchabala* after al-Khwarizmi's treatise) did the use of Hindu–Arabic notation and algebra begin to spread through Europe, checked at every point by vehement resistance from the Church and the guilds. When, in the same century that the *Liber abaci* appeared, the prophetic philosopher Roger Bacon (c. 1214–92) attempted to promote Hindu–Arabic mathematics as the foundation for all science, the key to a university education and a necessary study for theologians (who, he believed, ought 'to abound in the power of numbering'), he was accused by the Church of magic and condemned to life imprisonment. René Descartes (1596–1650) would argue something similar four centuries later and revolutionise European philosophy.

But while scholarly Europe rejected and even outlawed Hindu–Arabic learning, the new mathematics found a ready audience among the merchants of Italy, where it became known as 'abbaco' mathematics. According to Pacioli, 'abbaco' derived from either a corrupted form of *'modo arabico'* (Arabic style) or a Greek word, because it had little to do with the abacus. In fact, it was a method of calculation that made the abacus redundant. Abbaco made possible what we now take for granted: the adding, subtracting, multiplying and dividing of Hindu–Arabic numerals on paper with a pen, rather than the old two-part system which used counters on a board to calculate a sum and then recorded the result in Roman numerals, leaving no written trace of the calculation made. Fibonacci's *Liber abaci* spawned an alternate education system to the Latin-based monastery schools of Italy:

the abbaco schools, intended for the sons of merchants, who were taught Hindu–Arabic mathematics and learnt to read and write in their native tongues, an innovation that would encourage both the codification and standardisation of the vernacular languages of Europe, and the demise of Latin as the language of scholarship. By 1338 Florence had six of these abbaco schools for boys aged eleven and older who aspired to trade (very few girls attended school). Through these schools Italy's population became one of the best educated in Europe.

The teachers of these budding merchants were called 'abbacists' and many wrote their own vernacular textbooks based on the problems and solutions contained in Fibonacci's Latin *Liber abaci*. This major and influential mathematical tradition, to which Luca Pacioli belonged, was virtually unknown to historians until the 1960s, when some 288 abbaco manuscripts dating from 1290 to 1600, and 153 printed abbaco treatises, most of which deal with algebra, were discovered in Italian archives. As well as introducing Hindu–Arabic notation to centuries of Italian schoolboys and giving rules for addition, subtraction, multiplication and division, these treatises included general rules for solving common commercial problems such as discount, partnership divisions, barter and currency exchange, mostly using the Rule of Three—and in doing so they took mathematics beyond the privileged enclave of clergy, scholars and the nobility to the people. Abbaco mathematics would unleash first a cultural revolution—by making possible the mathematics of perspective, it transformed Italian art, sculpture and architecture in the fifteenth century—and ultimately a revolution in science, through its focus on the mathematical observation and measuring of nature rather than its idealisation.

While abbaco mathematics was transforming the way generations of Italian merchants and artisans understood the mechanics of commerce and the material world, in the rarefied atmosphere of the European universities—which began to emerge around 1100 in Paris, Bologna, Salerno, Oxford and Cambridge—mathematical techniques were regarded mostly as fictions. They could provide useful information for computing such things as heavenly positions to determine the dates for celebrating Easter and other Christian festivals, but no more. In complete contrast to the abbaco tradition, university mathematics was not considered to be a language for use in daily life. It was taught as 'astrology'—even in the 1510s Pacioli was referred to as 'astrologer' to Pope Leo X, and as late as 1598 the professor of mathematics at Pisa was required to lecture on astrology—and only in around 1400 did it begin very slowly to become an independent university discipline to be studied for its own sake, and for its broader application to the physical world. And not until the mid 1500s had astrology been renamed 'mathematics' in all the universities of Italy except in Ferrara.

The education of Luca Pacioli

So where does the 'father of accounting' fit into this divided stream of Italian mathematics and education? Pacioli would have attended his local communal school, which was already well established by the end of the fourteenth century—set up and paid for by the town to teach its sons reading, writing and grammar. Each year about one hundred boys from the ages of six to fifteen attended Sansepolcro's communal school, which quickly assumed a vital role in maintaining the order of town life, and especially in managing its children. This is made clear in a letter dated 20 November 1392 in which the townspeople—'everyone of the land of San Sepolcro'—made the following appeal to the ruling Malatesta lord: 'we have always customarily had a salaried foreign master of grammar, good and sufficient who was paid through your financial official in the quantity of 42 florins per year'. But the latest master had not been paid properly and had left. 'Due to this our children and our little ones devalue themselves and have become evil. How useful it is to the community of the territories to have a master of grammar; and how damaging and defective it is not to have one should be clear and manifest to Our Magnificent Lord.'

As a student in Sansepolcro after its takeover by Florence, Pacioli would have been taught the remnants of the old medieval scholasticism, based on the quadrivium and trivium of Boethius, as well as the new Florentine

Humanism. There is no surviving record of an abbaco school or master in Sansepolcro, but whatever mathematics Pacioli was able to glean during his boyhood in the town, probably through his apprenticeship with Folco de' Belfolci, it was enough to inspire him to devote his entire life to its study. Here he was introduced to a new and agile system of notation, Hindu–Arabic numerals, which simultaneously made and recorded mathematical calculations—and he must have been struck by the sheer power and magic of articulation he was suddenly capable of.

Inscrutable to most Europeans only five hundred years ago, Hindu–Arabic mathematics seems so 'normal' to us today—our civilisation depends upon it—that we forget the enormity of the revolution required to establish it as the norm and thereby to produce our mathematical, quantitative approach to reality. Pacioli lived through the early decades of the morphing of Italian mathematics from medieval Roman to a fusion of Hindu–Arabic and Greek, and its application to every area of fifteenth-century life, notably those two most famous to us in the twenty-first century: Renaissance painting and architecture. It was abbaco mathematics that made possible in the 1430s Brunelleschi's celebrated dome of the Cathedral of Santa Maria del Fiore, which still dominates the skyline of Florence almost six hundred years later. And Sansepolcro was the home of one of the century's greatest exponents of the new mathematics, Piero della Francesca. Known in his day as much for his genius as a mathematician as for his talent as a painter, Piero wrote three treatises on mathematics: *Trattato d'abaco*, an abbaco treatise; *De prospectiva pingendi*, on the application of maths to painting; and *Libellus de quinque corporibus regularibus*, his attempt to reduce all visual appearance to five key three-dimensional geometric shapes—known as the Platonic solids—which were believed to symbolise divine perfection and order. As was typical in those fledgling days of print, his treatises were never published in printed form but remained in manuscript, held in the library of Piero's friend the Duke of Urbino.

Although Piero was long assumed to have been Pacioli's teacher, recent scholarship has found no record of his ever having been a teacher, let alone teaching mathematics to Pacioli. Whatever the case, before Pacioli left Sansepolcro for Venice in 1464 to become an abbaco teacher, he had absorbed the lessons of Piero della Francesca, either directly as a student or indirectly through Piero's influence on the culture of the town. Pacioli later based much of his own work on Piero's treatises and reproduced parts of them verbatim, as he sometimes acknowledges: 'And in this treatise I promise to give you a full knowledge of perspective by means of the documents of our countryman and contemporary the master of his field Magister Petro de Franceschi, who has already prepared a very valuable compendium on this subject which we well understand . . .' And for this reason the two men's names have been permanently joined in the annals of history, starting with Giorgio Vasari's *Lives of the Most Eminent Painters, Sculptors and Architects*, published in 1550. Vasari devotes a chapter of his *Lives of the Most Eminent Painters* to Piero della Francesca—and mentions in only his second paragraph the monk Luca Pacioli (as 'Fra Luca del Borgo'). With several strokes of his quill Vasari bound the two men together for all time, writing:

> The man who should have tried his best to increase Piero's glory and reputation (since he had learned everything he knew from him), instead wickedly and maliciously sought to remove his teacher Piero's name and usurp for himself the honour due to Piero alone by publishing under his own name—that is, Fra Luca del Borgo—all the efforts of that good old man who, besides excelling in the sciences mentioned above, also excelled in painting.

Vasari continues with his praise of Piero and his damnation of Pacioli. The quality of Piero's books 'is so excellent that they have quite deservedly acquired for Piero the reputation of the greatest geometrician who lived in his times', and yet his student Pacioli, Vasari claims, passed them off as his own work. It was Vasari who started the rumour that Pacioli had been Piero's student.

The first and only book-length biography of Pacioli—*No Royal Road: Luca Pacioli and his times* (1942) by

R. Emmett Taylor—elaborates on Vasari's version of the story. According to Taylor, it was Piero 'who awakened in Pacioli a desire to put mathematics to work by taking it out of libraries, where it had slumbered so long, and to use it in everyday life'. Among the scraps of evidence given by historians for their alleged relationship is Piero's inclusion of a portrait of Pacioli in his mysterious Montefeltro altarpiece now in Milan, the *Madonna and Child with Saints* commissioned by Federico da Montefeltro of Urbino. Here Pacioli is said to appear as the Dominican Saint Peter Martyr, the second saint from the right, portrayed with his characteristic and distinctive head wound still bleeding (Saint Peter Martyr was killed by a blow to the head in 1252 by an assassin hired by two Venetians). That this is Pacioli's portrait is a widely held and plausible view, first proposed by an Italian historian and maintained by the rigorous economic historian Basil Yamey, who is not given to flights of fancy. The face of Saint Peter Martyr in this portrait does bear a striking resemblance to the only official portrait of Pacioli: both share the same dark hair, hooded eyes, set mouth with thin lips and strong, jowly jaw.

What is clear, however, from the trajectory of Pacioli's life is that he had a gift for developing relationships with prominent or influential men, especially the leading artists of his day, including the painters Gentile and Giovanni Bellini, Sandro Botticelli, Domenico Ghirlandaio, Pietro Perugino and Leonardo da Vinci, and so it is possible that he sought out Piero in Sansepolcro. But although Pacioli refers to Piero several times in his work as his fellow countryman (*conterraneo*), he never calls him his teacher and it is more likely that he came across Piero's mathematics in the library of Urbino after Piero's death in 1492. Regardless of the nature of their relationship, Piero and his mathematics were central to Pacioli's own life and work—and regardless of how he acquired it, the young Pacioli was armed with a knowledge of abbaco mathematics when he set off to seek his fortune in the New York of fifteenth-century Europe: Venice.

LUCA PACIOLI: FROM SANSEPOLCRO TO CELEBRITY

... learn multiplication from the root from
Maestro Luca

LEONARDO DA VINCI, LIST OF 'THINGS TO DO', C. 1495

We know a poet like Homer, an orator like
Demosthenes, a philosopher like Aristotle, but
first of all the entire Italian world deems it right to
know the Brother [Luca Pacioli] for restoring the
arithmetical science.

DANIELE CAETANI OF CREMONA, 1509

IN 1464, AGED NINETEEN, LUCA PACIOLI LEFT THE small market town of Sansepolcro and travelled east along ruined Roman roads frequented by outcasts and outlaws to one of the largest and most cosmopolitan cities in Europe—Venice. Writer Jan Morris conjures its moody environs well: 'This damp expanse, speckled with islets, clogged with mudbanks and half-drowned fields, protected from the sea by its narrow strands—this place of beautiful desolation is the Venetian lagoon.' Presiding over the realm where lagoon meets Grand Canal is the former power centre of the Venetian Republic, the Doge's Palace, an architectural fusion of east and west described by Ruskin as the central building of the world. Further along the Grand Canal stands the Rialto, the Wall Street of Pacioli's age. Here the first state bank of Europe was opened in the twelfth century. For the next three hundred years the Rialto dominated international currency exchanges from England to Egypt. In the late thirteenth century the Venetian *ducato*—ducat or 'coin of the dukedom'—usurped Florence's *fiorino* to become the monetary standard of trade throughout the known world. In 1472, the Venetian Senate attested to its significance when it declared 'the moneys of our dominion are the sinews, nay even the soul, of this republic'. The ducat was protected above all else and anyone caught violating it was severely punished: those who debased the ducat had their right hand cut off; men caught coining were blinded, while women had their noses cut off.

It was a commercial dominance Venice still enjoyed when the teenage Pacioli first beheld its magnificence. By the 1460s the population of Venice was about 150,000, making it the third largest city on the Continent, after Paris and Naples. For the moment Venice still held sway over the Mediterranean, despite the relatively recent conquest by the Ottoman Turks of its major trading hub—Constantinople—in 1453. Unlike the other Italian city-states, Venice put the demands of commerce high above the rule of the Church. One year after the Turkish defeat of Constantinople, the Venetian Republic signed a peace treaty with the Ottoman Empire, the enemy of Christendom, and continued business as usual—that is, when they were not embroiled in one of their many clashes. For its forbidden trade with the infidel, Venice incurred the wrath of the Pope and was excommunicated several times during the fifteenth century.

Pragmatism was the guiding principle of Venice and had brought it stupendous wealth and power. Its rise to commercial prominence began in the ninth century, founded on its favourable terms of trade with the Byzantine Empire; its monopoly of salt, a commodity then more desirable than gold for its ability to preserve food; and its rule of the waves. Venice's relationship with the sea was so essential to its survival that it was celebrated annually in an elaborate wedding ceremony. For eight centuries from 997 the city of Venice, in the person of its ruler the Doge, married the Adriatic Sea; every year on Ascension Day the Doge sailed across the lagoon in full wedding regalia to the entrance to the Adriatic and tossed a diamond ring into its briny depths, vowing: 'O sea, we wed thee in sign of our true and everlasting dominion.'

The might of Venice was built on such seamless bindings of spiritual ritual with commercial advantage and political pragmatism. Even the tale of her ruling saint, Mark the Evangelist, said to have been shipwrecked in the lagoon, is in fact a story of subterfuge and mercantile opportunism. Saint Mark's mummified body was stolen from a church in Alexandria in 828 by two Venetian merchants and presented to the Doge in his new palace— and thus became the patron saint of Venice, usurping its original and all but forgotten Saint Theodore. The abduction of Saint Mark, a superior saint to Theodore, signified the city's growing independence and influence. Its rule was further extended in 1203 when its 88-year-old Doge, Enrico Dandolo, diverted a group of pilgrims heading peacefully to the Holy Land and tricked them into conquering Constantinople for Venice instead. They returned with a haul of Byzantine treasure, including the four bronze horses now in the Museum of San Marco, and so the foundations of the Venetian maritime empire and its prodigious wealth were laid.

Venice controlled the mercantile traffic of Constantinople until 1453. The busy life of one Venetian merchant based in Constantinople before its sacking, Jachomo Badoer, is preserved in the pages of his ledger, the only commercial document to have survived the city's destruction in its entirety. Just as the books of Francesco Datini of Prato are cutting-edge fourteenth-century commercial practice, so the innovative Badoer is an exemplar of the fifteenth-century Venetian businessman. Written from 1436 to 1439 entirely in the new Hindu–Arabic numerals, Badoer's ledger is an invaluable record of Venetian mercantile life and of the hectic commercial activity of the Levant.

Badoer was a nobleman who for over three years ran a commercial venture in Constantinople, the meeting place of the trade routes of Europe and Asia, trading for himself and as an agent for Venetian merchants. In the busy bazaars of Constantinople he bought spices, incense, leather, wool and slaves to ship back to Venice for his brother to sell on the Venetian market. The first two weeks of November and June were always Badoer's busiest times, because it was then that his fleet prepared for its return trip to Italy, in compliance with the Venetian Senate, which required merchants to return to Venice at Christmas time and again in July to ensure a regular marketing of goods in the city. To escape the daily grind of the Byzantine marketplace, Badoer rented a villa in the suburbs of Pera, a Genoese colony on the coast nearby.

Venetian trade was closely controlled by the Senate, and the four galleys Badoer took to Constantinople were armed and probably accompanied by warships. The dangers of sea travel—including natural disasters and the 'Turkish peril'—led to the development of maritime insurance, an industry new in Badoer's day and one into which he ventured. Charging a premium of 3 to 19 per cent (depending on the risk factor), Badoer suffered only one insurance loss over three years, a testament to the protection provided by the Venetian navy to its merchants.

On reaching Constantinople, Badoer spent his first week unloading his wares and distributing the bills of exchange he had brought from Venice. The bill of exchange (*lettera di cambio*) and the bank transfer (*scritta di banco*) were the two credit instruments of Renaissance businessmen and served their interests very well. One took care of fund transfers between merchants living in different cities and the other of fund transfers within a local market. The bill of exchange was widely used in Renaissance finance. Its primary purpose was to allow the transfer of funds between resident merchants and their foreign agents without the risks involved in shipping gold or other precious assets. It also served as a borrowing medium. Badoer charged a commission of 1 per cent for honouring these bills and made no attempt to disguise the interest payments, as was usual in Renaissance finance due to the Church's opposition to usury.

In defiance of official Church policy, Venetian attitudes to interest rates were closer to our own: they considered it legitimate to borrow money at interest as long as it was determined by the market and was practised openly. If the interest rate was reasonable, around 5 to 8 per cent, the Venetian courts would enforce the collection of a contract. To honour his bills of exchange, Badoer had at least four accounts with local bankers in Constantinople, where banking was organised along the same lines as on the Rialto: a bank's primary function was not to lend money, but to transfer the funds of its depositors, who personally presented themselves to authorise the transfer of money to creditor accounts in different cities.

Most importantly, Badoer kept his books using a system that was essentially double entry, despite its inaccuracies (for example, his ledger does not balance exactly). His ledger, which mainly recorded accounts receivable and accounts payable, shows debits on the left-hand page and credits on the facing page, a two-column system that was the hallmark of Venetian double entry and is still used today. But unlike today's accountants, Badoer was not concerned with problems of valuation: he recorded his acquisitions of merchandise at cost using market value or, when the transaction was not made with money in the marketplace (barter was still common), estimated money values. He also used a profit and loss account to record his net income so he could regularly assess the health of his business. As in many of the early ledgers, the entries in Badoer's ledger are in paragraph form, with a rough column of monetary values in the right-hand margin denominated in Byzantine money. Badoer's use of Byzantine currency entailed constant conversion between Venetian ducats and Turkish *asperi*, calculations he made using the ever-fluctuating exchange rates determined at the Rialto; this invaluable information was conveyed to him via his regular correspondence with Venice. The Rialto's busy foreign exchange market provided regular exchange-rate updates for the many currency conversions carried out daily in Venice, the centre of international trade.

So successful did the merchants of Venice become that by the fourteenth century, traders were travelling across Europe to the Rialto—and sending their sons—to learn from their expertise in the commercial arts, especially abbaco arithmetic, currency exchange and their famous bookkeeping system. Merchants arrived from Germany in such great numbers that a five-storey complex—known as the Fondaco dei Tedeschi, or 'trading post of the Germans'—was built near the Rialto to accommodate them. And so it was natural that an ambitious young man such as Luca Pacioli, with a flair for abbaco mathematics, should seek his fortune in Venice.

When Pacioli arrived in Venice in the 1460s, its immense wealth was mired in decadence, the stink of its canals was disguised by incense, perfumes and spices, and its inhabitants were afflicted with malaria, the plague and a pervasive lassitude. A celebrated Venetian physician of the day attributed their ill health to sexual excesses, gluttony, a sedentary life and sudden changes in temperature. The choir of San Marco was known throughout Europe and music filled the streets. Bands as we know them today had just become fashionable and frenzied dancing was common. The Piazza San Marco had been given a new look: a Byzantine-styled entrance had recently been added to the Doge's Palace to proclaim Venice's position as the major power between Christendom and the east—and to distract attention from the increasing threat posed by the Ottoman Empire to Venice's command of the eastern Mediterranean. The renovation included the gradual repainting of 22 frescoes in the palazzo's Great Council Chambers, work assigned to the Venetian artist Gentile Bellini. His absence from the job in the next decade (in 1479) was a sign of the times: in that year the Doge lent Gentile to the Ottoman Sultan Mehmed II for two years, as part of the terms of a peace treaty between Venice and the Ottoman Empire.

The teenage Pacioli travelled to Venice to take up a post as tutor and abbaco teacher to the three sons of a wealthy fur merchant, Ser Antonio de Rompiasi, and he seized every opportunity that Venice offered. He continued his mathematical studies and gained valuable commercial experience working as an agent for Rompiasi, who was based on the Giudecca, an island south of Venice proper. It had originally been a place of banishment and, later, the first settlement of Jews (hence its name), but by the fifteenth century it had become a fashionable and highly desirable Venetian district. Two decades later in 1487, when he was writing his great mathematical encyclopaedia in Perugia, Pacioli remembered Rompiasi and his sons fondly. Referring to his first written work (now lost)—an abbaco text from 1470 dedicated to the three brothers—Pacioli wrote of his 'illustrious pupils, the brothers Bartolo and Francesco and Paolo de Rompiasi of the Giudecca, worthy merchants in Venice, sons of Ser Antonio, within their paternal and fraternal shadow, I found shelter, in their own house'.

Pacioli lived with the family on the Giudecca and his primary duty was to teach Rompiasi's teenage sons arithmetic and bookkeeping to equip them for the family business. He also took advantage of Venice's pre-eminence in mathematical studies, attending its Scuola di Rialto, a school founded in 1408 which attracted students from across Europe wanting to learn mathematics, astronomy, theology and natural philosophy, and where Pacioli studied under Domenico Bragadino, Venice's public reader in mathematics. In a practice dating from 1433, official professors and lecturers in Venice were well paid by the state (from rates levied on house rents and business profits) and so academic positions there were highly sought after. Venice was also the first Italian city to endow public lectures in algebra, and Pacioli would himself return to the Scuola di Rialto forty years later to lecture in mathematics. In his role as agent for Rompiasi's maritime business, Pacioli travelled throughout the Adriatic and perhaps as far afield as Greece and the Holy Land.

Leon Battista Alberti and the Eternal City

~

Most importantly, while working with Rompiasi, Pacioli learnt bookkeeping Venetian-style, a priceless skill he took with him when he left Venice, and Rompiasi's service, to travel to Rome with Leon Battista Alberti in 1470. How Pacioli met Alberti, the great Florentine Humanist, history does not tell, but Alberti now became Pacioli's trusted mentor and guide to the inner sanctum of the Eternal City.

Rome was then a city of ruins with a population of no more than 60,000, a small provincial town whose outlying suburbs had returned to nature. But it was the centre of the most powerful European institution of the day, the Church. And Alberti, as a member of its administration (in 1471 he was Secretary to the Papal Chancery), was in a position to introduce Pacioli to the men who ruled it, including Pope Paul II, his successor Sixtus IV, and Sixtus's nephew Giuliano della Rovere, who became Pope Julius II in 1503 and who would become Pacioli's patron. (The Renaissance system of patronage formed one of its primary webs of socio-economic relationships, essential not only for artists but for anyone who aspired to worldly success. Pacioli was fortunate throughout his life in his patrons, who gave him financial support, protection, favours and access to networks of powerful men.)

Historian Jacob Burckhardt called Alberti the first universal genius—and his was a genius of both body and mind. Alberti was intellectually brilliant, physically beautiful and an outstanding athlete. According to his autobiography, which he wrote in the third person around 1438, he could 'with feet tied, leap over a standing man; could in the great cathedral [the Basilica di Santa Maria del Fiore in Florence] throw a coin far up to ring against the vault' and he 'amused himself by taming wild horses and climbing mountains'. Such self-praise was common in the Renaissance and Alberti's was well founded. A leading Humanist thinker accomplished in mathematics and passionately devoted to its application to art, architecture and daily life, he was also one of the first to understand the enormous potential of the printing press (invented in Europe in the 1450s) and of writing in the vernacular, an understanding he passed on to Pacioli. Alberti was the first to formulate the mathematics of perspective to explain to painters how they could achieve a naturalistic illusion of depth in their work—or, in other words, convey on a flat surface the impression of three dimensions. In 1435 he published his method in Latin as *De pictura* ('On Painting'), the first ever treatise on the theory of painting. (It was published in the vernacular the following year.) The new method of perspective painting would be taken up by Piero della Francesca and Leonardo da Vinci, taught by Pacioli, and would revolutionise Italian art.

Departing radically from medieval thought, Alberti also valued material wealth. He expressed a respect for money that was new in Europe and would characterise his century, distinguishing it from the Middle Ages, an era when money was scarce, peasants were the majority, barter was the primary mode of exchange, people lived largely on what they or their village could produce, and wealth was seen as an obstacle to salvation. Money, wrote Alberti in the 1430s, is 'the root of all things': 'with money one can have a town house or a villa; and all the trades and craftsmen will toil like servants for the man who has money. He who has none goes without everything, and money is required for every purpose.' As historian Fernand Braudel argues, something new enters European consciousness in Alberti's writing—along with his celebration of money went thriftiness and a concern with the value of time, 'all good bourgeois principles in the first flush of their youth'. This radically new attitude towards wealth in the Renaissance is rarely remembered today, when we celebrate almost exclusively its artistic flowering.

Already contemplating his mathematical encyclopaedia, Pacioli was drawn to Rome by the prospect of working in the Vatican library. Built by Pope Nicholas V (1397–1455) with Alberti's guidance, by 1455 the Vatican library had the largest collection of manuscripts in Europe, greatly enhanced by the fall of Constantinople two years earlier, which prompted an influx into Italy of Greek scholars and manuscripts, especially the works of ancient Greek science and mathematics. As a result, in the 1470s Pacioli could access most of the texts of Greek and Arabic mathematics, which were available for the first time to scholars in Italy in the celebrated Renaissance libraries of Rome, Florence, Venice, Milan and Urbino.

AN ITINERANT MATHEMATICIAN

When Alberti died in 1472, Pacioli left Rome for Naples, another large centre of learning and Greek scholarship.

He found work as a merchant and an abbaco teacher before leaving for Perugia two years later—and thus began his life as an itinerant teacher. Pacioli became a travelling salesman for Hindu–Arabic mathematics and spent the rest of his life wandering across Italy, teaching first as an abbaco master and later at universities as professor of mathematics.

Because Italy was a series of warring city-states at the time, such extensive travels were dangerous unless you travelled with the protection of the Church. With its sanction, monks could journey unmolested and find accommodation almost anywhere. Perhaps for this reason—and for the career opportunities offered by the Church—soon after leaving Rome Pacioli took the vows of a Franciscan friar. By 1475 he had joined the Conventual Franciscans, the division to which his new patron Giuliano della Rovere and the then Pope (Sixtus IV) both belonged, and which was influential in Sansepolcro. The Conventuals were the most liberal variety of Franciscans and allowed Pacioli to teach mathematics and travel about the countryside with almost as much freedom as a layman. And because of his mathematical accomplishments and powerful friends in the Church, Pacioli was also granted special exemptions from several rules of his brotherhood, especially those regarding the ownership of property (according to the will he left behind, Pacioli died a wealthy man).

In Perugia, Pacioli embarked on his great work, the *Summa de arithmetica, geometria, proportione et proportionalità*, the first encyclopaedia of all the mathematics known in Europe at the time, which synthesised the three major mathematical traditions he had inherited: medieval European mathematics, Arab mathematics and the ancient Greek sources, which had recently arrived in Europe from Constantinople. To support himself he worked as an abbaco teacher. Perugia's city council appointed Pacioli first as a public lecturer in abbaco arithmetic and later in geometry as well. He gave his lessons in Latin to a class of about one hundred and fifty students who spoke a range of Italian dialects and foreign languages.

In December 1477 Pacioli began work on the second (and only surviving) of his three unpublished abbaco textbooks for his pupils, *Tractatus methematicus ad discipulos perusinos* ('Mathematics Treatise for the Students of Perugia'), which he finished the following April. It includes a section on mercantile tariffs which Pacioli copied from elsewhere without acknowledgement. This provides an instructive context in which to see his borrowings in the *Summa* and subsequent charges of plagiarism, such as those levelled by Vasari: borrowing without attribution was a regular and acceptable practice in the abbaco tradition in which Pacioli worked. There were no readily available texts for abbaco teachers and so they wrote their own, copying other texts which were all ultimately sourced in Fibonacci's *Liber abaci*. Only when these texts began to be printed following the spread of the printing press in Italy in the late 1470s did questions of copyright—and therefore of plagiarism—begin to arise.

In 1481 Pacioli left Perugia for Zara, a city now in Croatia but then the capital of the Venetian territory of Dalmatia, where he wrote his third and most advanced abbaco text for his students. When he returned to Italy, Pacioli took his masters degree in theology, a course which at the time included mathematics, and by 1484 he had attained the highest academic rank of the day, 'magister', or master. This qualified him to teach mathematics at university level, which was better paid than abbaco teaching. There were thirteen universities in Italy in Pacioli's day and each one employed only one or two mathematicians, but Pacioli would be appointed the first chair of mathematics at two of them (those of Perugia and Rome). Pacioli's combined training in both abbaco and university mathematics was extremely rare. Only two other mathematicians in the whole of Renaissance Italy are known to have possessed similar expertise and training.

Continuing his research for the *Summa*, Pacioli spent much of the early 1480s in Florence, immersing himself in the mathematics available in the splendid Medici Public Library. He praised the library for its excellent mathematical manuscripts, including Witelo's *Perspectiva*, a key thirteenth-century treatise on optics based on the work of the eminent Arab mathematician Ibn al-Haytham, which was an essential source for the mathematics of artificial perspective used by Renaissance painters such as Piero della Francesca. In Florence,

Pacioli also met and befriended many of the leading artists and sculptors of the day, including Botticelli, who had recently returned from Rome, where he had been among the artists painting the frescoes on the walls of the Sistine Chapel.

In 1486, Pacioli was appointed professor of mathematics in Perugia. Like any twenty-first-century academic, he writes of these years as burdened with the demands of teaching while he attempted to write: 'If I do not seem to have treated these questions properly, I pray that they may correct my way of speaking and have pity on one who feels other worries, as I feel the burden of daily reading, lecturing and teaching, here in this beloved august City of Perugia.' When his contract at the University of Perugia expired, Pacioli returned to his birth town for the first time in seventeen years.

Home with his fellow Franciscans, Pacioli immediately fell out with his monastery's authorities: in 1491 he had a heated disagreement with the head of the Conventual Franciscans and was nearly excommunicated from the order. Exactly what this disagreement was about is not known, but it may have related to a complaint made about Pacioli to the order in the same year, which led the Franciscans to forbid the monk to teach the young men of Sansepolcro. This hazy episode has prompted speculation about Pacioli's possible homosexuality, fuelled by his long intimacy with Leonardo da Vinci during the 1490s.

Otherwise, Pacioli spent this time in Sansepolcro

quietly finishing his manuscript on everything that was known about mathematics in 1490s Italy. He was lucky to have one of the best libraries in Europe nearby, over the hills to the east in Urbino. The library had been built up by the bookish Duke of Urbino, Guidobaldo, a friend of Pacioli and the son of Federico da Montefeltro (he who commissioned the famous Montefeltro altarpiece from Piero della Francesca mentioned earlier). A renowned intellectual, Guidobaldo had collected most of the important mathematical manuscripts of the age, including Jacobus Cremonensis' translation of Archimedes, the *Algebra* of al-Khwarizmi, and Piero della Francesca's *De quinque corporibus*. These works—along with Fibonacci's *Liber abaci*—formed the basis of Pacioli's two bestselling books, the *Summa* and *De divina proportione* ('The Divine Proportion', on the golden ratio).

In 1494, encouraged by his friends and his new patron Marco Sanuto, Fra Luca Pacioli was ready to publish the sum of his learning.

PACIOLI AND THE PRINTING PRESS
~

And so, aged 49, Pacioli travelled to Venice for the second time, to take advantage of the new opportunities opened up by the recently arrived printing press for those with written material to offer the public. In Pacioli's case, the material was the culmination of his life's work so far: his mathematical encyclopaedia, *Summa de arithmetica, geometria, proportione et proportion-alità.* As we have seen, Pacioli had by now achieved a distinction that was almost unique in fifteenth-century Italy: he was an experienced teacher in both commercial (abbaco) and speculative (university) mathematics. He had also spent six years as a merchant's assistant in the busiest trading centre in Europe, and he had for almost twenty years been studying the entire body of mathematics known to the Mediterranean of his day: the rediscovered work of the ancient Greeks, the Latin mathematics of the medieval schoolmen and the advances of the Arabs. The hefty manuscript he brought with him to Venice contained this collected mathematical knowledge, based largely on Euclid's *Elements* and the work of Fibonacci. His manuscript would become the first printed book to deal with Hindu–Arabic arithmetic and its offshoot, algebra, and contain the first printed treatise on Venetian bookkeeping. These two great contributions to the scientific and commercial life of Europe—its transmission of algebra and of double-entry bookkeeping—make the *Summa* the work for which Pacioli is now remembered.

As the leading mathematician of the moment, Pacioli was able to find both a patron to fund the printing of his enormous manuscript and a printer in Venice who was willing to publish it. The printer was Paganino de Paganini, who had set up his printing shop in Venice in 1483 when the new communications technology was becoming well established in the city. Although printing had been invented three decades earlier in Germany—probably by a Mainz metalworker, Johann Gutenberg—the art of printing numbers and figures accurately and efficiently had only been invented the year before Paganini opened his press. The German printer Erhard Ratdolt, who was based in Venice—the up-and-coming centre of the new industry—had noticed that while many works of the ancients were printed in Venice, almost nothing mathematical had appeared because there was no way of reproducing figures. And so Ratdolt devised a way to reproduce tables of figures and other mathematical symbols accurately and in 1482 printed the first mathematics text of the Humanist programme—Euclid's *Elements*.

Four years earlier in 1478, the Venetian Republic had produced one of the earliest known printed books on mathematics, an abbaco treatise in the vernacular known as the *Treviso Arithmetic*. It is a telling moment in the history of printing: Humanists had been demanding a printed edition of Euclid, but the first printed mathematics book was for merchants, not scholars. Commercial imperatives and practical necessity drove the early printers' decisions about which books to publish as much as the competing agenda of scholars and the Church, much to the outrage of Humanists such as the celebrated Erasmus of Rotterdam. While making extensive use of printing to disseminate his own work, Erasmus was scandalised by the fact that so soon after its invention, the press had escaped the control of scholars and fallen into the hands of merchants and business-men. Pacioli's mentor Leon Battista Alberti was one of the first to understand the revolutionary significance of the new technology. Writing in Rome in the 1460s, Alberti gives a sense of the quantum leap in communications that printing provided: 'we greatly approved the German inventor who in these times has made it possible, by certain pressings down of characters, to have more than two hundred volumes written out in a hundred days from an original, with the labour of no more than three men; for with only one downwards pressure a large sheet is written out.'

The first book printed in Venice (Cicero's *Epistolae ad familiares*, an ancient Roman classic) had been published in 1469. But the printing houses of Venice struggled to find a market for their unwieldy printed 'manuscripts' of classics and religious works, and within five years nine of Venice's twelve printers had gone bust. It seemed the new technology was not commercially viable. But the merchant bankers of Venice thought otherwise. They soon realised the commercial potential of printed books and invested the large sums required to keep the printing presses running. To the merchants of Venice, the printed book was simply a commodity like any other and could be sold along the trade routes of Europe like pepper, silk, wax and other luxury goods. Venice became the centre of the new communications technology, the Silicon Valley of the Renaissance, and many of the first printed works on business and commerce were published in the city on the lagoon.

By the time Pacioli returned in 1494, Venice had become the publishing capital of southern Europe, with more than 268 printing shops run mostly by experts from Germany and France. They came to Venice because of its favourable business conditions: its large labour force, low printing costs, stable liberal government run by merchants for merchants, readily available patronage, and its vigorous intellectual community which could provide the translators, proofreaders and scholarly advisors that a successful printing press required. The time- and labour-saving advantages of the printing press were huge compared to the old medieval communications technology of manuscripts handwritten by scribes. For example, in 1483 the Ripoli Press charged three times as much for setting up and printing a translation of Plato's *Dialogues* as a scribe did for duplicating the same work. But the press produced 1025 copies, the scribe one copy, making printed books more than 300 times cheaper than manuscripts. Books rapidly became widely available and affordable to a new class of readers; in 1500 the price of a book in Venice was about a week's salary for a teacher or a skilled artisan, equivalent to the price of a good desktop computer today.

The printing press created an explosion in demand for multiple copies of instruction manuals and texts for students and teachers—and their sudden availability to a wide audience helped to break down the culture of secrecy that had prevailed in medieval Europe, spawned by the guilds, who were more concerned with guarding their trade secrets than with publicising their knowledge and technical skills. With the printing press came an 'avalanche' of how-to books (similar to the many hundreds of DIY books published each year today), explaining the previously arcane arts of everything from playing musical instruments to keeping accounts in double entry.

This enthusiasm for the new technology was particularly pronounced among Renaissance mathematicians, who, according to historian Paul Lawrence Rose, were possessed of an 'almost missionary faith' in the power of the printing press to spread knowledge. Pacioli was one who led the way into this new world. Far from considering vernacular translations beneath him, and despite being fluent in Latin, Pacioli broke with scholarly tradition and wrote his encyclopaedia in Italian, the language of the people. He also encouraged the use of the new mathematics and its Hindu–Arabic numerals, lamenting those merchants who still used Roman numerals and the old methods in their arithmetic. His *Summa* was emblematic of the new printing programmes.

As was typical in these early days of printing, Pacioli stayed in Venice during the printing of his encyclopaedia, visiting Paganini's print shop daily to correct and add new material to his manuscript as it went to press. The initial print run, estimated to have been around two thousand copies, would have taken from nine to twelve months to complete, at a rate of one sheet of paper (or two pages) per day of the 615-page book. Pacioli writes in the *Summa* of its production, saying that he worked day and night with 'industry in the workshop of that clever man Paganino de Paganini', correcting his manuscript with his own hand.

THE *SUMMA DE ARITHMETICA, GEOMETRIA, PROPORTIONE ET PROPORTIONALITÀ*

~

The printing of the *Summa* was funded by Pacioli's patron Marco Sanuto, a professor of mathematics from a famous patrician family whose intellect, virtue and thoughtful generosity Pacioli praises at length in his introduction. With an eye to eternity, he says that Sanuto had made 'this volume of mine possible so that it may be handed down to posterity'.

But Pacioli dedicated the *Summa* to the Duke of Urbino, Guidobaldo da Montefeltro, whose library he had used for his mathematical researches and who may also have been Pacioli's student at one time. In his dedication to the duke, Pacioli outlines his intentions for his work, which were revolutionary at a time when books were written in Latin and destined for a cloistered scholarly elite. Rather, the *Summa* is written in the language of the people so it can be read by 'each and every man' and used in everyday life. Pacioli tells the duke that he has written this book because he 'desire[s] to be of use' to Guidobaldo's subjects. And he takes great pains to stress that although 'I am not ignorant of eloquent style, and realise that you should be addressed with a wave of eloquence since you are so learned in Ciceronian eloquence', he has decided to write his encyclopaedia in the vernacular 'because if this were written in Latin each and every man could not understand it. I have written it so that it may bring advantage and pleasure to those who in literature are learned or not.'

Mathematics, says Pacioli, applies to almost every human activity, from astrology, cosmography and theology, architecture, painting, sculpture and music, to business, law and military strategy. 'Why, the citadels of states, the walls of cities, the towers, trenches, ramparts, mounds, and all of the other defensive and offensive weapons of war are nothing else but geometry and proportion,' says Pacioli, giving the example of Archimedes' famous defence of Syracuse from the Romans with his mathematical knowledge, which he used to build weapons including a huge crane. Known as the 'Claw of Archimedes', it allegedly lifted enemy boats out of the harbour and upturned them, drowning all their warriors. Pacioli concludes by saying that 'if you examine carefully each one of the other sciences and liberal arts there is not one which does not use in some way harmony, measure, and proportion'. According to him, without these three mathematical properties 'everything ceases to exist'.

The *Summa*'s title and introduction are in Latin but the main text is in the Florentine vernacular, an Italian dotted with Latin and Greek words and abbreviations, and expressions from the local dialect, which was comprehensible to a large audience of merchants, businessmen, students, artists and technicians, as well as the more broadminded scholars otherwise used to reading in Latin.

Pacioli deliberately championed the vernacular not only because 'the subject matter will bear more fruit if there are more people to read it' but also because, as he was the first to understand, Latin was not at all suited to explicating mathematics. To make his prose as clear as possible for his readers, Pacioli also took his images and analogies from daily life. For example, he explains eight different ways of multiplying. The sixth method was generally known as the square, cell, sieve or net, because of the way the numbers were set out on the page. But Pacioli called it the '*gelosia*', because, as he says, 'the arrangement of the work resembles a lattice or "*gelosia*". By *gelosia* we understand the grating which it is the custom to place at the windows of houses where young ladies or nuns reside, so they cannot easily be seen. Many such abound in the noble city of Venice.' This passage, with its image and anecdote inspired by the everyday sights of Venice, is typical of Pacioli's mathematics.

The *Summa* is divided into two volumes, but all known surviving copies—estimated to be 162 copies—except one are bound into one book. Volume I contains nine chapters: chapters 1 to 7 cover arithmetic; Chapter 8 is the first systematic exposition in the vernacular of algebra; Chapter 9, on commerce, is divided into twelve sections, the first ten on matters such as barter and bills of exchange, the eleventh on bookkeeping, the twelfth on exchange rates and weights and measures. Much of the first volume was derived from Fibonacci. Volume II of the *Summa* contains one chapter only, which is the first printed vernacular text on geometry, summarising and updating the work of Archimedes, Euclid, Fibonacci, Benedetto de Firenze and Piero della Francesca. During his years in Venice in the 1460s, Pacioli had discovered a copy of Fibonacci's long-neglected *Liber abaci* in a monastery and immediately understood its value. By translating large sections of Fibonacci into the vernacular and including them in the *Summa*, Pacioli restored this seminal work to European mathematics.

Pacioli's famous bookkeeping treatise—Volume I, Chapter 9, Part 11 of the *Summa*—is so central to any history of double-entry bookkeeping that it requires detailed attention and will be discussed separately in the next chapter. But before we leave the *Summa* behind, it is worth noting its most significant contributions to European mathematics.

Pacioli introduced Hindu–Arabic numerals and their basic arithmetic to a wide audience in Italy for the first time. He explained the rules for working with these new numerals—for example, for addition, subtraction, division, fractions and roots—as well as including multiplication tables and examples of the many different ways of multiplying, such as the '*gelosia*' method mentioned above. In the fifteenth century, multiplication with numerals was considered to be extremely difficult, and division almost impossible, an art to be attempted only by experts. Pacioli also invented two new symbols, one for plus and one for minus, which became standard notation in Italian Renaissance mathematics (although they are not the symbols we use today).

Most importantly, the *Summa* was the first vernacular book printed in Europe to contain algebra—and it marks a dramatic departure from the algebra of the abbaco tradition. The *Summa* moves from using algebra as a means of solving specific problems to algebra as a language for making abstract arguments; Pacioli generalises algebraic derivations and formulates them as universally valid theorems. The extensive use of the *Summa* by sixteenth-century algebraists helped to lay the foundations of the scientific revolution and thus of modern science. Among the mathematicians who drew on the *Summa* were Nicholas Tartaglia (1500–57), who, with just fifteen days of schooling, wrote a treatise on arithmetic (1556) and numbers (published posthumously in 1560), and the notorious Girolamo Cardan (1501–76), a gambler and possible murderer obsessed with scandal, astrology and philosophy, whose *Ars magna* (1545) on algebra was the most advanced work of its day.

The *Summa* also contains the first printed text on the mathematics of linear perspective for Renaissance artists and architects, based on the work of Piero della Francesca. Pacioli acknowledges this in his dedication, when he mentions Piero's 'copious work which he composed on the art of painting and on the force of the line in perspective' which is in the duke's library in Urbino.

PUBLICATION

Pacioli's *Summa de arithmetica, geometria, proportione et proportionalità* was published in Venice on 20 November 1494, becoming the first mathematical encyclopaedia of the Renaissance and one of the earliest books to be printed on the Gutenberg press. Given that it includes the entire mathematical and commercial knowledge of his age, Pacioli's encyclopaedia is correspondingly massive. Even for its time, when big books were popular with wealthy bookbuyers for their apparent gravitas and resemblance to manuscripts (which were considered more valuable than printed books), the *Summa* was an exceptionally large book. It measures 25 by 30 centimetres and runs to 615 densely printed pages, the equivalent of a 1500-page textbook if it were typeset today. The *Summa* is also widely considered to be one of the most beautiful of all the early printed books. The 1494 edition in the library of Sansepolcro is leather-bound and metal-studded. Inside, its pages are tissue thin, its print is stark and the capital letters of its gothic font are decorated with woodcuts of Fra Luca dressed in monk's robes and holding a compass. In its margins are explanatory graphs, diagrams and computations.

Priced at 119 soldi, the *Summa* was expensive (the popular *Aesop's Fables* was only two soldi) but well within the means of the wealthy merchants, artisans and nobles of Venice, Florence, Milan and other Italian cities. It was a commercial success, selling steadily over several decades and making its author famous. Highly unusually in those early days of print when intellectual copyright was a new concept, Pacioli was given a ten-year copyright on the initial publication and in 1508 he petitioned the Venetian Senate for a twenty-year copyright on any reprint of the original 1494 edition, which he was granted. This made him one of the first writers to be granted literary copyright. Ten years after the *Summa* was first published, Pacioli's bookkeeping treatise was extracted and published separately by Paganino de Paganini in Tuscany as *La scuola perfetta dei mercanti* ('The Perfect School of Merchants'), under Pacioli's name.

A second edition of the complete *Summa* was published in 1523 at Toscolano on Lake Garda and paid for by the printers. This edition was greeted by an even more receptive public—and only then was Pacioli widely lauded, posthumously (he died in 1517), for having dared to write in the language of the people. The *Summa* became the most widely read mathematical work in Italy for a century and trained several generations of readers in mathematics and bookkeeping.

CELEBRITY

~

The publication of the *Summa* brought Luca Pacioli fame throughout Italy and he was given one of the greatest honours of the age: his portrait was commissioned. Pacioli became the first mathematician in Europe of whom we have an authentic portrait, and probably the first mathematician ever to have a portrait painted. The *Portrait of Fra Luca Pacioli* was painted in Venice, probably in 1495 by Jacopo de' Barbari, and now hangs in the Galleria Nazionale di Capodimonte in Naples. It shows Pacioli dressed in grey Franciscan monk's robes, demonstrating a mathematical problem. One hand points to a diagram drawn in chalk on a slate, the other rests on the page of an open manuscript, next to which is a big red book, probably the *Summa*, and a wooden model of a dodecahedron (one of the five Platonic solids, solid polyhedra whose faces are all identical regular polygons, such as a cube).

Beside Pacioli stands a young auburn-haired man long believed to have been Guidobaldo, the Duke of Urbino, especially as the portrait is dedicated to him. But recently an English mathematician, Nick Mackinnon, analysed the portrait, which he believes depicts a real geometry lesson, to claim that the young man is in fact the German artist and future mathematician, Albrecht Dürer, who was in Venice in 1495 seeking the secrets of the new Italian painting. Mackinnon thus argues—persuasively—that Pacioli's portrait 'captures one of the greatest moments of the Renaissance, the transmission to Albrecht Dürer, and hence to the world north of the Alps, of the geometry of Ancient Greece and the basis of the new art of Italy'. If he is right, then Pacioli played a pivotal role not only in the history of mathematics and commerce, but also in the history of European art.

MILAN

Soon after the portrait was painted, Pacioli left Venice for Milan, where a 42-year-old engineer and master of theatrical spectaculars had bought a copy of the *Summa* in 1494 for its arithmetic and treatise on linear perspective. At the insistence of this engineer, Pacioli was summonsed to the Court of Milan by its ambitious ruler Ludovico Sforza. Inspired by the Medici in Florence, Ludovico was in the midst of transforming his realm into a true Renaissance city, a centre of the arts and learning complete with a court of intellectuals. As part of his modernisation, he had recently introduced mathematics lectures, and in 1496 he invited Luca Pacioli to take up Milan's first Chair of Mathematics.

The engineer responsible for Pacioli's move to Milan was Leonardo da Vinci, who had arrived in the city fourteen years earlier. Vasari says that Leonardo was first presented to the Milanese court not as an engineer nor even as a painter but as a musician, and 'took with him a lyre that he had made himself, mostly of silver, in the shape of a horse's skull, a very strange and novel design which made the sound fuller and more resonant'. But Leonardo was keener to promote himself to Ludovico as a military engineer, a more highly esteemed profession, writing in his letter of introduction: 'In short, I can contrive an infinite variety of machines for attack or defence', including cannons, armoured cars, siege-machines, tunnel borers and bridges. Only as an aside does Leonardo mention that 'in painting I can do everything that it is possible to do'.

When Pacioli met Leonardo in Ludovico's Castello Sforza in 1496, the artist was preoccupied with mechanics, hydraulics, architecture and engineering. According to an anonymous source, Leonardo was 'of a fine person, well proportioned, full of grace and of a beautiful aspect. He wore a rose coloured tunic, short to the knee, although long garments were then in fashion. He had, reaching down to the middle of his breast, a fine beard, curled and well kept.' The two men were obsessed with arithmetic and geometry, believing, as Leonardo put it, that they embraced 'all the things in the universe', that without them 'nothing can be done'.

At the time, Leonardo was working on two ambitious art projects: a huge equestrian sculpture in bronze to honour Ludovico's father (which was never cast), and a giant fresco in the church of Santa Maria delle Grazie, about ten minutes' walk from the Castello Sforza. The church and its buildings were being completely remodelled by Ludovico to glorify the Sforza dynasty, and Leonardo had been commissioned to paint the monks' dining room with the subject traditionally used for refectories: the Last Supper. As with everything he did, Leonardo's approach to the fresco was scientific. He had taught himself arithmetic from Pacioli's *Summa* and now Pacioli himself was in Milan to help Leonardo with the mathematics of linear perspective for the creation of his hyper-real *Last Supper*. On its completion in 1498, the *Last Supper* caused an immediate sensation, with Pacioli one of the first to praise it. Leonardo's fresco was widely copied in a range of sizes and, then as now, visitors to Milan (including the King of France) rushed to see it. In his own treatise on art, Leonardo calls perspective 'the subtlest investigation and invention of the mathematical studies which, by force of lines makes remote that which is near and large that which is small'.

THE WORLD'S OLDEST MAGIC TEXT

During his three years in Milan, Luca Pacioli collaborated with Leonardo da Vinci on several projects, including his next book, *De divina proportione*, which he dedicated to Ludovico Sforza. Although Pacioli finished *De divina proportione* in 1498, he did not have it printed for another eleven years: his busy life at the court of Milan was brought to an abrupt end with the invasion of the city in October 1499 by the army of Louis XII of France, who took the Castello Sforza. It is said that French soldiers dragged Pacioli from his lodgings at the nearby San Simpliciano monastery and destroyed his mathematical models, believing they were the work of the devil. Pacioli escaped Milan with Leonardo and together they made their way to Mantua, where Isabella d'Este (whose sister Beatrice was married to Ludovico) was receiving refugees from the Milanese court. In gratitude, Pacioli dedicated a second book he had been working on in Milan to Isabella and her husband, the Marquis of Mantua. The book—called *De viribus quantitatis* ('On the Powers of Numbers')—was a compendium of magic, recreational mathematics and proverbs. It was not published during Pacioli's lifetime and was not published until 1997, having languished for five hundred years in the Bologna University Library.

Like most of Pacioli's work, it was written in the vernacular. The first of its three sections is the earliest known comprehensive collection of mathematical games and problems, such as the famous conundrum faced by a man with (in Pacioli's version) a 'wolf, a goat and a bundle of cabbage' who wants to cross a river in his boat, which is only big enough to take himself and one other item at a time. The second section is a range of puzzles and jests, from card tricks and instructions on how to write a sentence on the petals of a rose to how to wash your hands in molten lead—Pacioli explains that you must soak your hands in cool well water, shake them, and then you are ready to put them in a pan of molten lead over a flame: it will not cook you and 'it will appear to be a miracle'. (This trick was tested by Adam Savage and Jamie Hyneman in the 2009 season finale of

MythBusters and amazingly they found it worked with lead heated to 450°C.) The third section is a collection of proverbs and verses, including 22 riddles.

VENICE AND THE GOLDEN RATIO

After leaving Isabella d'Este's refuge in Mantua in late 1499, Pacioli shared a house with Leonardo da Vinci in Florence and worked as a professor of mathematics at its university. He then returned to Venice in 1508 to supervise the printing of *De divina proportione* and his Latin translation of Euclid's *Elements*. But before he embarked on his second great printing programme, on 11 August 1508 Pacioli gave an introductory lecture on the fifth book of Euclid at the church of San Bartolomeo near the Rialto Bridge. Some five hundred people came to hear the celebrated mathematician speak, including architects, printers, ambassadors, magistrates, theologians, artists and philosophers. The famous Venetian printer Aldus Manutius was there and may have brought along Erasmus, who was staying with him near the Rialto while supervising the printing of his translations of Euripides and a collection of ancient proverbs. Intriguingly, after leaving Italy in 1509 Erasmus wrote his famous satire, *In Praise of Folly*, in which he mocks scientists who use maths to bamboozle their audience. His description of these boffins rather accurately parodies the methods used by Luca Pacioli in his talk on Euclid: 'When they especially disdain the vulgar crowd is when they bring out their triangles, quadrangles, circles, and mathematical pictures of the sort, lay one upon the other, intertwine them into a maze, then deploy some letters as if in line of battle, and presently do it over in reverse order—and all to involve the uninitiated in darkness.' In his book, Erasmus set out to deflate the pretensions of anyone who claimed special knowledge or importance, whether they were philosophers, merchants or clerics.

If Erasmus did have Pacioli in his sights here, then in this particular instance it was probably not without reason. Although Pacioli generally aimed to bring mathematics to the widest possible audience in the most accessible way, he was also prone to flights of fancy, especially when he attempted to conflate mathematics with Christianity. He told the crowd that Euclid's Book V on proportion was one of the most difficult sections of the *Elements* and that proportion 'is the quality which alone penetrates the inmost being of the most high and undivided Trinity', just the sort of remark that might have prompted a deflating barb from Erasmus.

The following year, Pacioli was back in the printing shop of Paganino de Paganini, printing his Latin edition of Euclid and *De divina proportione*. According to Pacioli, *De divina proportione* was inspired by the fervent discussions which regularly erupted in Ludovico Sforza's court about the application of mathematics and natural science to art, a subject of crucial importance in the Renaissance. In response, Pacioli had decided to write a book which explained the mathematical basis of the arts for 'everyone who loves to study philosophy, perspective, painting, sculpture, architecture, music and other mathematical disciplines'.

In his dedication of *De divina proportione* to Ludovico, Pacioli assures him that his esoteric mathematical speculations are 'no old women's tales, no false and ludicrous jestings, no lying and unreliable poetic imaginings, which please the ears only with empty vapours'. But despite Pacioli's declaration of its practical purposes, *De divina proportione* is also his most mystical work. It concerns the 'divine proportion'—better known today as *phi*, or the golden mean or ratio—and its relation to the five Platonic solids. The golden ratio—which results when a line is divided so that the short portion relates to the longer portion as the longer relates to the whole—is intimately interconnected with the Fibonacci sequence and likewise recurs with uncanny frequency throughout the natural world, including in the human body (for example, the navel divides the body according to the golden ratio); in the spiral growth of shells; the proportions of a dolphin's eye, fins and tail to its body; and the seed heads of a sunflower.

Leonardo made a set of 60 beautiful geometric drawings for *De divina*, which Pacioli acknowledges in his dedication. Thanks to Leonardo's illustrations, its powerful patrons and its accessibility, *De divina proportione* became the best known and most successful of all Pacioli's books in his day.

MAD QUEEN'S CHESS

~

Pacioli claimed to have written one more book—*De ludo scacchorum*, rumoured to have been the first book on chess—which many doubted ever existed because no copy had been found. But Pacioli's claim was confirmed in 2006 when a copy was discovered in a library in northwestern Italy. While Pacioli was travelling from city to city teaching abbaco in the 1470s a new style of chess was spreading through southern Europe, characterised by the dramatically enhanced powers of the queen and bishop and extended powers for the pawns. Because it made the queen the most powerful piece on the board, it was called 'mad queen's chess'—*scacchi alla rabiosa*—and quickly became popular in the courts of Italy. Pacioli's book on the subject contains over a hundred chess problems and instructions, including how the new powers of the queen, bishop and pawn worked on the board.

The rediscovery of Pacioli's *De ludo scacchorum* ('Of the Game of Chess') excited interest mostly because of its possible connection to Leonardo da Vinci (who probably made its futuristic black and red illustrations). But the book is significant in the context of Pacioli's life because it clearly shows the vast range of his interests as a mathematician as well as the depth of his intellect. Some of the puzzles it contains are so complex and sophisticated that they have been attributed to Leonardo, a known genius. While it is most likely that Leonardo was involved in this project—it was probably compiled around 1500 when the two men were together in the court of Isabella d'Este, a noted chess player—it is more likely that Pacioli himself was the intellect behind the puzzles.

Pacioli's last years

~

After seeing his Euclid and *De divina proportione* through the press in Venice, Pacioli returned to Sansepolcro at the end of 1509. In welcome, the attentive friars of his monastery filed a complaint against him to the general of the Franciscan order, arguing that not only had he failed to abide by the vows of poverty required by the Franciscans, but that 'this Master Luca', far from being a model monk fit to direct others, 'according to what we understand and see daily, is a man who ought to be corrected'. The head of the Franciscan monastery in Sansepolcro asked that Pacioli be deprived of his papal favours and all administrative duties. History does not record the details of Pacioli's misdemeanours and much has been speculated on their nature, for example, that with his cosmopolitan lifestyle, fame and mathematical genius, Pacioli had lorded himself over his less learned brothers in his provincial home town. Or, that his reprehensible behaviour was of a more scandalous nature, pertaining to sexual and other worldly indulgences. Whatever it was about Pacioli that had caused the complaint to be made, it was soon dropped—and in reply, less than three months later, on 22 February 1510, Pacioli was appointed head of the monastery in Sansepolcro by the general of the Order of Conventual Franciscans.

In 1514, Pacioli accepted his final academic appointment, as professor of mathematics at the University of Rome. His listing on the university's faculty roll is the last record we have of him. He died a few years later, probably in 1517.

Pacioli's contemporary Daniele Caetani of Cremona expresses an early sixteenth-century view of the monk's achievements, focusing on his exceptional gift for collecting, organising, simplifying and making available the mathematical knowledge of the Renaissance:

> The science of mathematics, after being hidden
> in speculation and conjecture, what was not
> practical because so many of the bodies had
> been reduced to various and complex figures,
> Lucas alone of many rendered simple by
> explanation, so that even the very ignorant
> could understand just as if he had set it forth
> under their very eyes. And who in former
> times ever dared to make this very notable
> beginning? Surely no one, not even the most
> learned mathematician before Lucas Paciolus,
> who was in this respect a man of the rarest
> pattern and almost unique.

Pacioli became famous in his day for his knowledge of mathematics, his gift for systemising, formulating and updating it, and his passion for disseminating its secrets via the printing press to the widest possible audience in their own tongue. But his lasting fame would rest on his 27-page bookkeeping treatise, *Particularis de computis et scripturis*—and it is to this work that we now turn.

4

PACIOLI'S LANDMARK BOOKKEEPING TREATISE OF 1494

Right is the proverb which says, More skills are
required to make a successful businessman than
are required to make a good lawyer.

LUCA PACIOLI, 1494

[Pacioli's bookkeeping treatise,] that prized Italian
book . . . has influenced us to such an extent that
the principles it enunciates as of use in its day,
remain the foundation of our present methods of
bookkeeping.

JOHN B. GEIJSBEEK, 1914

TODAY LUCA PACIOLI IS BEST KNOWN FOR ONE SMALL
part of his *Summa de arithmetica, geometria, proportione et proportionalità*—a 27-page, 24,000-word
bookkeeping treatise called *Particularis de computis et
scripturis* ('Particulars of Reckonings and Writings').
De computis is the only significant part of the *Summa* to

have been translated into English, as well as some fourteen other languages, including Dutch, German, French and Russian.

As we shall see, because of the power of the printing press to spread multiple copies of identical texts relatively cheaply and quickly (compared to the scribal culture that preceded it), Pacioli's bookkeeping treatise, as the first printed synthesis of the method, gradually made Venetian bookkeeping the standard across Europe. Delving into Pacioli's original not only gives us a good grasp of the basics of his bookkeeping practice and of the world of the fifteenth-century Italian merchant, but also an insight into how uncannily and unexpectedly close they are to our own.

PACIOLI'S DOUBLE ENTRY

~

As with the rest of the *Summa*, Pacioli begins *De computis* by dedicating it to Guidobaldo, Duke of Urbino. According to Pacioli, he wrote this 'special treatise which is much needed' with the duke's subjects in mind. Pacioli hopes to give the citizens of Urbino enough bookkeeping rules to enable them to keep their accounts in an orderly way—and possibly also to ensure that their businesses flourish and therefore incur higher taxes for their ruler to collect.

Pacioli defines double-entry bookkeeping broadly, as 'nothing else than the expression in writing of the arrangement of [a merchant's] affairs'. If a merchant follows the system Pacioli sets out, then he will always know 'all about his business and will know exactly whether his business goes well or not. Therefore the proverb: If you are in business and do not know all about it, your money will go like flies—That is, you will lose it.'

Pacioli's formulation of Venetian double-entry bookkeeping is one of the great advances in the history of business and commerce. He recommends this method, which had been practised in Venice for two hundred years, as the best: 'This treatise will adopt the system used in Venice, which is certainly recommended above all the others, for by means of this one, one can find his way in any other.' Rather than mingling debit and credit entries under each other down a single column or page—as did the Florentine merchants before they began keeping their books *alla viniziana*—Venetian ledgers separate debits and credits, dividing them into two columns, which is exactly how we organise our ledgers today. As Pacioli says, this is the most important thing to note in Venetian bookkeeping: 'All the creditors must appear in the Ledger at the right hand side, and all the debtors at the left. All entries made in the Ledger have to be double entries—that is, if you make one creditor, you must make someone debtor.' The word debit comes from the Latin *debere*, to owe; the word credit from the Latin *credere*, to believe.

In Pacioli's view, three things are needed by 'anyone who wishes to carry on business carefully. The most important of these is cash or any equivalent, according to that saying, Without this, business can hardly be carried on.' The second thing necessary in business 'is to be a good bookkeeper and ready mathematician'. The third 'and last thing is to arrange all the transactions in such a systematic way that one may understand each one of them at a glance, ie, by the debit and credit method'. Not much has changed today. A prudent person wishing to set up a business needs cash, a decent bookkeeper and a sound double-entry bookkeeping system (mostly these days provided by accounting software packages).

Pacioli does not go into great detail, as he makes clear in his introduction: 'Although one cannot write out every essential detail for all cases, nevertheless a careful mind will be able, from what is given, to make the application to any particular case.' Nor does he give sample pages of worked examples, as writers on bookkeeping would begin to do in the next century. Instead, he assumes his readers are merchants and their sons, with some working knowledge of bookkeeping.

As far as Pacioli is concerned, systematic bookkeeping is the key to a merchant's peace of mind. He says Venetian double entry 'is very essential to merchants, because, without making the entries systematically it would be impossible to conduct their business, for they would have no rest and their minds would be always troubled'. Ever the teacher, as well as praising the value of Venetian bookkeeping, Pacioli frequently interrupts *De computis* to extol the virtues of merchants or offer concerned advice. He counsels merchants to work hard and not to rest in bed, for they face many challenges 'on the sea, on land, in times of peace and abundance and times of war and famine, in times of health or pestilence'. A merchant must remain ever vigilant: 'In these crises he must know what to do, in the marketplaces and in the fairs which are held now in one place and now in another. For this reason it is right to say that the merchant is like a rooster, which of all the animals is the most alert and in winter and summer keeps his night vigils and never rests.'

By the fifteenth century, the marketplaces Pacioli mentions had spread across Europe and the Mediterranean and were dealing in a wealth of goods: Cotswolds wool exchanged in London; silver, copper, iron and tin from the mines of central and eastern Europe; furs from Russia, Siberia and Bulgaria; carpets, brocades, silks and spices traded in centres such as Cairo, Alexandria, Constantinople, Damascus and Tabriz. The fairs he mentions had proliferated in Europe during the twelfth and thirteenth centuries. The most famous were the annual trade fairs of Champagne in northeastern France, where textiles, furs, leather and spices were bought and sold. And today's Frankfurt Book Fair, held annually in October, had its origins in an autumn trade fair formally established in 1240 by the German king, Frederick II.

Among Pacioli's words of advice is his recommendation that merchants dedicate all their account books to God. He says 'merchants should begin their business with the name of God at the beginning of every book and have His holy name in their minds' and mark their first account book 'with that glorious sign from which every enemy of the spiritual flees and before which all infernal spirits justly tremble—that is, the holy cross'.

Here we see the complex relationship that existed between religion, business and bookkeeping in the early Renaissance world, when commerce was a morally questionable pursuit and making a gain from the clever management of money was frowned upon, hence the Church's ban on usury. (Such condemnations of usury date back at least to Aristotle, who said that interest was the vilest form of wealth-making because it 'makes a gain out of money itself and not from the natural object of it'.) As Francesco Datini of Prato did a century before, Pacioli advises merchants to incorporate explicit signs of Christianity into their books as a way of legitimising their profit-seeking activities. The use of double entry itself was like the Catholic confession: if a merchant confessed—or accounted for—all his worldly activities before God, then perhaps his sins would be absolved. These Christian flourishes that Pacioli recommends merchants include in their books are therefore no mere ornaments.

THE BASICS OF DOUBLE ENTRY
VENETIAN-STYLE

~

To teach the Venetian system of orderly bookkeeping, Pacioli says he will be using the example of someone starting out in business and taking his readers through the various procedures this merchant would need to undertake in order to set up his accounts, 'so that at a glance he may find each thing in its place'. And then—as he so frequently does in his bookkeeping treatise—Pacioli throws in a precaution and an adage drawn from his long experience working with Rompiasi in Venice and his many years teaching bookkeeping to the youth of Italy. He writes: 'For, if he does not know how to put each thing in its own place, he will find himself in great trouble and confusion as to all his affairs, according to the familiar saying, Where there is not order, there is confusion.'

In today's profit-driven commercial world we are more than familiar with the idea that the purpose of every business is to make a profit. But Pacioli was writing in an era when this was not so self-evident and the tools for calculating profit—especially the Venetian bookkeeping system—were not widely used. And so he makes it clear that the purpose of every merchant is 'to make a lawful and reasonable profit so as to keep up his business'.

The first thing a merchant must do, says Pacioli, is to make an inventory of everything he owns. A merchant 'must always put down on a sheet of paper or in a separate book whatever he has in this world, personal property or real estate, beginning with the things that are most valuable and most likely to be lost, such as cash, jewels, silver, etc'. And, as most businesses still do today, the Renaissance merchant must complete his inventory in one day, 'otherwise there will be trouble in the future in the management of the business'. Pacioli adds this warning because an inventory is a record of a business's stock holding as of a particular date or time period, and so the smaller the period during which it is conducted the more accurate the inventory will be.

In the sample inventory that Pacioli gives for a typical Venetian merchant on 8 November 1493, he lists a fantastic array of riches, including papal florins and cash in gold and coin from Venice, Hungary, Siena and Florence; cases of ginger, sacks of pepper, packages of cinnamon and cloves, sandalwood, fox and chamois skins; and a many-storeyed house with 'so many rooms, courtyard, wells, garden, etc, situated in St Apostle Street over the Canal'. He lists the merchant's bank deposits in various parishes of Venice and all their details, including the name of every clerk who served the merchant, 'so that you can easily find your account when you go to get money, because in such offices they must keep very many accounts on account of the big crowd that sometimes goes there'. To complete his inventory, the merchant must add the details of his debtors and of his own debts.

Once the inventory is made, a merchant needs three books in which to record his business transactions. The first is the *memoriale*, or memorandum, which acted like a diary and was also known as a 'waste book' because it was a temporary record of the merchant's transactions. Pacioli describes the memorandum as 'a book in which the merchant shall put down all his transactions, small or big, as they take place, day by day, hour by hour'. In this book the merchant must record the details of 'everything that he sells or buys, and every other transaction without leaving out a jot; who, what, when, where, mentioning everything to make it fully as clear as I have already said in talking about the Inventory'.

The second book required is the *giornale*, or journal. After entering his inventory into the journal, the merchant uses this book to write up in a neat and orderly fashion the details of each transaction that has been recorded in the memorandum. In Pacioli's Venetian system, every item entered into the journal must be preceded by one of two key words: *per* (which means 'from' and indicated that the ledger account must be debited) and *a* (which means 'to' and indicated that the ledger account must be credited). No item is ever entered in the journal unless it is preceded by one of these two expressions.

The third book is the *quaderno*, or ledger. The ledger is made up of pages ruled into two columns (the simplest form of which is now known as a T-column) and it records—twice—every journal entry. For every entry made in the journal there will be two in the ledger: one, a debit, entered on the left-hand side of the T-column; and the other, a credit, on the right. The ledger with its two columns marked a great advance in account-keeping. By using this system the merchant could at any moment see at a glance the precise state of his assets and his debts. It also allowed him to find mistakes in his bookkeeping relatively easily, because if his books did not balance—if his debits were not equal to his credits—he had made a mistake somewhere and would have to scrutinise his books to find it. The ledger with its 'double entries' in a bilateral account was an innovation made by the merchants of Venice and is the reason that Venetian bookkeeping is now known as double entry.

The merchant's books must be registered with a mercantile officer. Pacioli says that you should tell the officer 'that those are the books in which you intend to write down, or somebody else write down for you, all your transactions in an orderly way'. In addition, the officer must be told which kind of money you will be using to record your transactions. In an age when each major city had its own mint and its own currency, merchants had to choose with which of the myriad currencies then in circulation to denominate their accounts. Once this is done, the mercantile officer will authenticate the books, attaching a seal to them to make them legal documents that can be presented in court.

ENTERING THE INVENTORY IN THE JOURNAL
AND THE LEDGER

~

After entering his inventory into the memorandum, the merchant must record it in the journal, using as already mentioned the two words which were required for journal entries in fifteenth-century Venice, *per* and *a*. Each journal entry must start with the debtor (*per*) and then immediately after it the creditor, denoted by *a*. That the debtor be given first is one of the fundamental conventions of double entry. The two entries are entered together one after the other on the same line, separated from each other with two little slanting parallel lines, //.

Pacioli then describes how a merchant should enter his holdings of cash in the journal, using the expressions 'cash' and 'capital'. He says that cash is your 'pocket book' and capital is the entire amount of what you possess. Then, as now, capital was always creditor in all the principal journals and ledgers, and cash was always the debtor.

That capital is always creditor and cash is always debtor in the principal books is another convention of double-entry bookkeeping. While in accounting the terms debit and credit are easily defined—they simply denote the left- or right-hand side of an account—they are not so easy to apply. As any accounting student would know, their use is not intuitive and can be confusing. For example, bookkeeping students must learn that a debit entry in an asset or expense account increases those assets or expenses, and that a debit entry in a liabilities, equity or revenue account decreases those accounts. The reverse is true for credit entries in each of these cases. Sorting transactions into debits and credits is the bane of an accounting student's existence and writers after Pacioli would include lists of rules to show how this is done. The instructions Pacioli gives are much briefer.

So, to enter your cash holdings of, say, 12,000 ducats into the journal (using today's journal style rather than Pacioli's), you do as follows:

Journal entry

		Dr (Debit)	Cr (Credit)
8 November 1493	Cash	12,000	
	Capital		12,000

You continue to enter your inventory, with a debit to the item recorded and a credit to capital. For example, in the case of the Venetian merchant in 1493, the item accounts will include ginger, pepper, cinnamon, cloves, sandalwood, and so on. In Pacioli's method, if the merchant enters his pepper into the journal, the entry would be: '*Per* pepper // *A* capital', with the value of the pepper given in ducats. This denotes a debit to the pepper and a credit to capital of the ducat value of the pepper. To work out the value of each item of stock, Pacioli says, you simply give each thing its 'customary price'. In the name of profit, he advises merchants to make their prices 'rather higher than lower; for instance, if it seems to you that they are worth 20, you put down 24, so that you can make a larger profit'.

Once all the entries are made in the journal, they must be transferred—or posted—to the ledger. Because each entry must be entered into the ledger twice, the ledger is larger than the journal (it was also known as the *quaderno grande*, or 'big book') and needs an index (which Pacioli calls a 'finding key') in which the merchant writes the names of all debtors and creditors, and the number of their respective pages.

To begin, the merchant must enter his cash on the first page of the ledger. Pacioli shows how a merchant should write in the ledger 'the first entry of the cash in the debit column, and then the first entry of the capital in the credit column'. After writing an acknowledgement of Jesus and the date, the merchant should write as follows: debit cash account on 8 November, credit capital, of 12,000 ducats. The ledger entries will be as follows:

In the cash account

	Cash	
8 November 1493	12,000	

In the capital account

	Capital	
8 November 1493		12,000

After the debit and credit entries are made in the ledger, they are struck through in the journal and their ledger page numbers added in the margin. By doing this, the merchant can reconstruct his ledger from either the memorandum or the journal if the ledger is lost.

Once Pacioli has explained how to transfer inventory entries from the journal to the ledger for personal goods, including cash, he explains how to enter merchandise into the journal and ledger, using the example of ginger. With stocks of merchandise, the merchant 'must always have in mind their number, weights, measurements and values according to the different ways in which it is customary to make purchases or sales among merchants in the Rialto, or elsewhere'. In the journal the total value of the merchant's ginger stocks are recorded as '*Per* ginger (details of ginger stocks) // *A* capital (details of ginger stocks are given along with their total value in ducats)'.

Then, as Pacioli reminds us, 'you shall make two different entries in the Ledger; that is, one in the debit and the other in the credit'. So in the ledger the ginger account is debited ('Ginger in bulk, or so many packages, debit on November 8 per capital' with the ginger valued 'according to current prices' at so many ducats) and the capital account is credited with the same amount.

Pacioli remarks that the merchant must enter all his merchandise into the journal and ledger in this way without forgetting anything because 'the merchant must have a much better understanding of things than a butcher' (a trade essential to Renaissance life).

ENTERING A TRANSACTION

~

Pacioli then explains how to make an entry in the memorandum for a transaction, using the example of a merchant who buys twenty pieces of white cloth at 12 ducats each. The entry is made in the following way: 'On this day we have or I have bought from Mr Filippo d'Rufoni of Brescia, 20 pieces of white *bresciani*' (cloth from Brescia, a town west of Venice). As he says, a merchant must record every detail of each business transaction in the memorandum. In this case, the merchant will record the date and place of the transaction, the details of the items bought, the name of the person from whom they were bought, the nature of the sale (for example, whether it was made in cash or only partly in cash, partly made in barter, or made through a broker), and so on. As Pacioli says, in the memorandum 'nothing should be omitted'.

For this same Venetian merchant who buys twenty pieces of white cloth at 12 ducats apiece on 21 November 1493, here is how the journal and ledger entries would be made today, using Pacioli's system but, for clarity, today's notation.

Journal entry

		Dr (Debit)	Cr (Credit)
21 November 1493	Cloth	240	
	Cash		240

(Purchased 20 pieces of white cloth for cash)

The ledger entries would be as follows:

1. Debit the cloth account for the value of the cloth purchased.

Cloth		
8 November 1493	3000	
21 November 1493	240	

(Where 3000 is the value in ducats of cloth already in the merchant's inventory and 240 is the value of the cloth purchased on 21 November 1493.)

Once again, Pacioli stresses, it is essential to make two ledger entries for each entry in the journal: 'you must never make a credit entry without making the same entry with its respective amount in the debit. Upon this depends the obtaining of a trial balance [*bilancio*] of the Ledger.'

For the Venetian merchant who has purchased cloth, the second ledger entry must be made in the cash account, which is credited with the amount the merchant has spent on his purchase of white cloth.

2. Credit the cash account for the value of the cloth purchased.

Cash		
8 November 1493	12,000	
21 November 1493		240

(Where 12,000 ducats is the value of cash in the merchant's inventory and 240 is the value in ducats of the cloth purchased.)

After the purchase of twenty pieces of white cloth at 12 ducats each the Venetian merchant will have 3240 ducats worth of cloth and his cash holdings will be 11,760 ducats (or 12,000–240).

KEEPING ACCOUNTS WITH PUBLIC OFFICES, PARTNERSHIPS AND BANKS

Pacioli details how and why to keep accounts with public offices, such as the municipal loan bank in Venice. These accounts must be kept very clearly, with 'good written evidence as to debits and credits in the handwriting of the clerks in those institutions'. It is very important to keep track of these accounts, because, as Pacioli explains,

> in these offices they often change their clerks,
> and as each one of these clerks likes to keep
> the books in his own way, he is always blaming
> the previous clerks, saying that they did not
> keep the books in good order, and they are
> always trying to make you believe that their
> way is better than all the others, so that at
> times they mix up the accounts in the books
> of these offices in such way that they do not

correspond with anything. Woe to you if you
have anything to do with these people . . .
Maybe they mean well, nevertheless they may
show ignorance.

Nothing much has changed in five hundred years: clerks
come and go, and each one regards their own method as
the best and their predecessor as the source of all confusion or error.

In fifteenth-century Venice, if a broker did not record
each and every commercial transaction, he was fined
and dismissed. As Pacioli says: 'And justly the glorious
republic of Venice punishes them and their clerks who
should misbehave. I know of many who in the past years
have been heavily punished, and right they are in having
one officer whose only duty is to oversee all these officers
and their books whether they are well kept or not.'

In his treatise Pacioli explains the full scope of a merchant's affairs, from how to keep an account with the
exchange at the Rialto, to the details of accounting for
'well-known and peculiar mercantile customs of trading
and partnership'. These 'peculiar' customs are extremely
important commercial activities and include 'tradings,
partnerships, suggested business trips, trips on your
own ventures, commissions from others, drafts or bills
of exchange'. Pacioli recommends that merchants keep
these accounts separately from their main business so
that their respective profits and losses can be shown.
Merchants should keep a separate set of books for their

dealings with partners, using categories of 'partnership's cash' and 'partnership's capital' to distinguish them from the merchant's own entries.

Pacioli tells his readers how to keep accounts with banks—'which you can find nowadays in Venice, in Bruges, in Antwerp, Barcelona, and other places well known to the commercial world'—which must be kept with the greatest diligence. He says that bank accounts are useful because they offer greater security for your money—even if their clerks are unreliable—and also allow merchants to make daily payments to their creditors. 'If you put money in the bank, then you shall charge the bank or the owner or partners of the bank and shall credit your cash.' The journal entries should be, for example, '*Per* Bank of Lipamani // A cash to the value of the deposit'. Given the potential waywardness of clerks, Pacioli reminds merchants that they must ensure they receive a written record of every transaction from the bank. For withdrawals, a merchant should do the opposite, that is, 'charge your cash and credit the bank or owners of the bank for the amount withdrawn'.

THE PROFIT AND LOSS ACCOUNT

Next Pacioli turns to the profit and loss account, which is kept in the ledger only, not in the journal. As he explains, the amounts in this account 'originate from overs or shorts in the debits and credits, and not from actual transactions'—and so into this account 'other accounts in the Ledger have their remainders'. What Pacioli means here is that each ledger account must be balanced, and the figures added to either the debit or the credit side of the account to make it balance are the 'remainders'. So, for example, to balance his cloth account the Venetian merchant in the example will have a credit of 3240 ducats. That is, his cloth holdings are now 3240 ducats, which is the 'remainder' of the cloth account.

Pacioli shows how to open this account: if you have sustained a loss in a particular line of merchandise, then that account in your ledger would show less in the credit than in the debit. And so 'you will add the difference to the credit so as to make it balance'. The entry in the merchandise account is as follows: 'Credit, *per* Profit and Loss, the amount needed to balance the merchandise account'. Then you go to the profit and loss account and debit the same amount, as follows: 'Profit and Loss debit, on this day, to such and such loss sustained, so much— which has been entered in the credit of said merchandise account in order to balance it at page so and so.'

The opposite would be done if the account for this particular merchandise showed a profit instead of a loss; that is, more in the credit than in the debit. The merchant must do this for all his accounts with merchandise or other goods. And by doing this, as Pacioli says, 'you will see at a glance whether you are gaining or losing, and how much'. Once this is done, the profit and loss account must be 'transferred for its closing into the capital account, which is always the last in all the ledgers and is consequently the receptacle of all other accounts, as you will understand'.

Balancing a ledger entails a thorough and painstaking check of every ledger entry against the journal. Pacioli gives strict instructions for this procedure: 'if you want to do this well you shall do it with great diligence and order. That is, first you shall get a helper as you could hardly do it alone.' He recommends giving your helper the journal and taking the ledger yourself. Once all the accounts in the ledger and journal have been checked and it is found that the two books correspond in debit and credit, 'it will mean that all the accounts are correct and the entries entered correctly'.

CLOSING THE ACCOUNTS OF THE OLD LEDGER

To close all the accounts of the old ledger, which will allow him to prepare a trial balance, the merchant must start with the cash account. Pacioli advises merchants to close their books once a year, to check that they balance: 'it is always good to close the books each year, especially if you are in partnership with others. The proverb says: Frequent accounting makes for long friendship.' If in the trial balance the debit totals (summarised on the left) and the credit totals (summarised on the right) are equal, the ledger has been well kept and can be closed. If the totals are not equal then there is a mistake in the ledger—which Pacioli generously excuses with 'at times you cannot be so diligent that you are unable to make mistakes'—and it must be checked again.

All the ledger accounts—cash account, capital account, merchandise, personal property, real property, debtors, creditors, public officers, brokers, et cetera—should be closed into the profit and loss account. By closing all these entries into the profit and loss account the merchant will have closed all the ledger accounts. By then adding all the credit and debit entries in this account, 'you will be able to know what is your gain or loss, for with this balance all entries are equalized; the things that had to be deducted were deducted, and the things that had to be added were added proportionately in their respective places'. If this account shows more in the debit than in the credit, it means the merchant has lost this amount since he began his accounts. If the credit is more than the debit, it means that over this same period of time the merchant has made a gain, or profit.

The last step in this process is to close the amount of profit or loss into the capital account—the same account in which 'at the beginning of your management of your business, you entered the inventory of all your worldly goods'. If there is a loss—'from which state of affairs may God keep everyone who really lives as a good Christian'—it must be closed to the debit side of the capital account. If there is a profit, it is closed to the credit side of the capital account.

This is the climax of the double-entry method, the

moment at which the merchant will be able to tell at a glance how his business is faring. To check that the ledger has been well kept and can therefore be closed, the merchant must then summarise on a separate sheet of paper all the debit totals of the ledger and place them at the left, and summarise all the credit totals at the right. These two columns are then added, the first being the grand total of the debits, the second the grand total of the credits. If these two grand totals are equal, 'that is, if one is just as much as the other—that is, if those of the debit and those of the credit are alike—then you shall conclude that your Ledger was very well kept and closed'.

PACIOLI CONCLUDES

~

In closing, Pacioli reminds his readers how important it is to keep accounts, 'for, if you are not a good book-keeper in your business, you will go on groping like a blind man and meet great losses'. He concludes his treatise by saying: 'Therefore, take good care and make all efforts to be a good bookkeeper, such as I have shown you fully in this sublime work how to become one.' He then adds a summary of all the rules he has given, 'which no doubt will be very useful to you. And remember to pray God for me so that to His praise and glory I may always go on doing good.'

In these 27 pages of the *Summa* Pacioli was the first to codify Venetian bookkeeping—and because he used the latest communications technology, the printed book, to record and disseminate this important commercial information, it was his version of Italian bookkeeping that spread across Europe, as we shall see in the next chapter.

VENETIAN DOUBLE ENTRY GOES VIRAL

[Printing] brought about the most radical
transformation in the conditions of intellectual life
in the history of western civilization . . . its effects
were sooner or later felt in every department of
human life.

ELIZABETH EISENSTEIN, 1979

Book-keeping by Double Entry, or what is
commonly called the Italian method of Bookkeeping, is the art of keeping our accompts in such
a manner, as will . . . exhibit to us our neat gain or
loss upon each article we deal in, by which we are
instructed what branches to pursue, and which to
decline . . .

WARDHAUGH THOMPSON, 1777

THE PRINTING PRESS AND THOSE WHO USED IT USH-
ered in a revolution in the presentation and
distribution of knowledge on a scale not seen again
until the invention of the computer in the twentieth

century. The printing press not only reduced reliance on oral transmission and transformed written culture, but its ability to produce multiple copies of identical texts served to advertise widely the power of printing itself. It was its own best advertisement. Within a decade of its invention in the 1450s, news of the printing press had spread across Europe and by 1500 there were printing presses from England (1476) to the Ottoman Empire (1494). A new book published in Rome was available to readers in England in a matter of weeks.

Erhard Ratdolt's discovery of a way to accurately reproduce tables of figures and other mathematical symbols dealt the final blow to the old Roman numerals. It also marked the beginning of the demise of Latin as the universal language of Europe and its gradual replacement by the language of science, which, as Italian astronomer and philosopher Galileo pointed out in 1623, 'was neither Latin nor the vernacular, but numbers and figures, circles, triangles and squares'. It is worth noting just how radically the printing of multiple copies of reliable charts and figures influenced the course of western civilisation. For a start, as Galileo understood, it made possible the triumph of science and the rise of mathematics as the universal language. Simultaneously, it brought about the demise of the Bible and religion as the ultimate and uncontested source of truth. As historian Elizabeth Eisenstein argues, the changes printing brought 'provide the most plausible point of departure for explaining how confidence shifted from divine revelation to mathematical reasoning and man-made maps'. It turns out that what Leon Battista Alberti thought he was seeing in the early fifteenth century— the introduction of mathematics to the arts, to painting, sculpture and architecture, as expounded in his 1435 treatise on painting, *De pictura*—was in fact merely one localised example of the spread of mathematics through every sphere of life.

As a printed treatise for merchants, Luca Pacioli's *Particularis de computis et scripturis* was caught up in the tide of this printing revolution. Via its pages, Venetian bookkeeping spread across Europe—and business-men no longer had to travel to the Rialto to learn the secrets of Venetian commerce. All bookkeeping texts published in the sixteenth century in Italian, German, Dutch, French and English were based directly on Paci-oli's *De computis*—and these books in turn influenced more than one hundred and fifty works on double entry published across Europe by 1800, from Sweden (1646) to Denmark (1673), Portugal (1758), Norway (1775) and Russia (1783), which were also ultimately derived from Pacioli's original. While Pacioli's Venetian method was not the only—nor even the most common—account-ing system actually used, it was the system the texts and teachers advocated and the one that many larger mer-chants adopted.

The system of three principal books that Pacioli codified—memorandum (or waste book), journal and ledger—is described by all subsequent accounting texts.

The memorandum recorded details of daily business transactions in chronological order, which were posted to the journal, then reordered and formalised and entered twice—once as a debit and once as a credit—in the ledger. This process of abstraction was described well by the English writer John Mair in 1757:

> The *Ledger* is the *Waste-book* taken to pieces,
> and put together in another order: the
> transactions contained in both are the same,
> but recorded in a different manner. The *Waste-*
> *book* narrates things in a plain, simple, natural
> way, according to the order of time in which
> they were transacted; the *Ledger* contains the
> very same things, but artificially disposed, so
> as things of the same kind are classed together,
> and all the particular *items* and *articles*,
> belonging to the same subject are collected
> and united.

One of the first bookkeeping texts to follow Pacioli's was by Domenico Manzoni, published in Venice in 1540. It was no more than a reprint of Pacioli's *De computis*, but nowhere did Manzoni acknowledge Pacioli. He was, however, the first to include full examples of entries in the journal and ledger, adding to Pacioli's original text a list of three hundred transactions which are entered into a model set of account books. Manzoni's examples and the fact that his book was published in a much more convenient weight and size than Pacioli's enormous *Summa* made his work an easy reference for practising bookkeepers and it became so popular that it went through six or seven editions in forty years. From northern Italy double entry spread across the alps to the nearest inland trading centre, Nuremberg, where the first German work on bookkeeping—again a copy of Pacioli's—was published in 1537.

With the decline of Venice as a commercial power in the sixteenth century, the port of Antwerp (now in Belgium) became the centre of international trade and it was here that bookkeeping made its next great advances. In *Allegory of Commerce*, painted in 1585, the artist Jost Amman portrays Antwerp in its full commercial regalia, complete with the motifs of double entry—allegories of profit, capital and cash flow—and merchants busy at their account books. The first Dutch work on Italian bookkeeping was published in 1543: *New instruction and the demonstration of the praised art of ciphering* by the merchant Jan Ympyn Christoffels, who had spent twelve years working in Venice. Through Ympyn's book and its French (1543) and English (1547) translations, double entry became known throughout Europe as the 'Italian method'. Ympyn followed *De computis* closely, mentioning Luca Pacioli as 'Brother Lucas de Bargo'. The fact that Pacioli was afterwards frequently referred to by this incorrect version of his name suggests that Ympyn's work was widely read and referenced.

The most innovative Dutch writer on bookkeeping was the celebrated mathematician, engineer, inventor and bureaucrat Simon Stevin (1548–1620), who learnt double-entry bookkeeping as an apprentice in Antwerp. Stevin became minister of finances and chief engineer of the Netherlands, as well as the tutor and advisor to its governor Prince Maurice of Orange. At Stevin's instigation, Prince Maurice introduced double-entry bookkeeping to the administration of every local government in his territory and learnt mathematics and commerce from the two-volume work Stevin wrote for his instruction. The second volume (1605) contains a bookkeeping treatise, *Account-keeping for princes after the Italian Manner*, which Stevin wrote in the form of questions and answers that actually arose during the arguments Stevin had with the prince while teaching him the often counter-intuitive art of double-entry bookkeeping. (The first volume appeared three years later, in 1608.) Stevin had a high opinion of businessmen and their shrewd intelligence—and believed that a knowledge of the merchant's art of bookkeeping would help the prince to manage his estates more efficiently, as 'merchants are better informed than princes of the state of their affairs and are less defrauded by those in their employment'. Stevin also wrote one of the first treatises on governmental accounting.

Stevin was deeply influenced by Pacioli and Ympyn, and in turn shaped the thinking of his friend Richard Dafforne, who through his book *The Merchant's Mirrour* became a pioneer of bookkeeping texts in England. But the earliest work on double entry in England was published a century earlier in London in 1543: Hugh Oldcastle's *A profitable treatyce called the Instrument or Boke to learne to knowe the good order of kepying of the famouse reconynge called in Latyn Dare and Habere and in Englyshe Debitor and Creditor*. It is based on a selection from Pacioli's *De computis* and, given the date, was possibly an English translation of Ympyn. There are no surviving copies of Oldcastle's treatise, but it was reworked and extended by a London schoolmaster called John Mellis in his *A briefe instruction* published in 1588. Like so many in his day, Mellis had travelled and studied in the Netherlands, which had become the training ground for English merchants after the decline of Venice.

Richard Dafforne's *The Merchant's Mirrour* was published in London in 1636. While in Holland learning the secrets of the merchant's art, Dafforne had met Simon Stevin and come to understand the inestimable value of double entry. When he returned to London and discovered there was no decent treatise on the subject to be found in England—'alas, the small love that a great part of our merchants bear to this science, daunteth the Pen of Industry in our Teachers'—he decided to write his own. Modelled on Stevin's, Dafforne wrote his treatise as a series of questions and answers. Here he explains the cash account, with cash personified:

Q: Why make you Cash Debtor?
A: Because Cash (having received my money
unto it) is obliged to restore it again at my
pleasure: for Cash representeth (to me) a man,
to whom I (only upon confidence) have put my
money into his keeping; the which by reason
is obliged to render it back, or to give me an
account what is become of it: even so if Cash be
broken open, it giveth me notice what's become
of my money, else it would redound it wholly
back to me.

For a seventeenth-century accountant, 'cash' as an abstract concept was difficult to grasp, but 'Cash' seen as a person who is lent money by the proprietor made sense and fitted into the logic of regular bookkeeping practice which accounted for a merchant's various debtors and creditors. The early writers included in their books endless lists of possible transactions to teach students how to determine credits and debits in any bookkeeping problem they might face. Dafforne lists thirty rules of thumb to shed some light on the tricky problem of analysing transactions into credits and debits, the scourge of an accounting student's existence then as now:

First I will book some exquisite rules of aid,
very requisite in Trade's continuance, to be
learned without book—1. Whatsoever cometh
unto us (whether money or wares) for Proper,

Factorage, or Company account, the same is . . .
Debitor 1. Whatsoever goeth from us (whether
money or wares) for Proper, Factorage, or
Company account, the same is . . . *Creditor.*

These lists of rules and examples used by the early
bookkeeping teachers and authors were gradually
replaced during the nineteenth century by the analysis
of bookkeeping practices, when the first signs of modern transaction analysis—the examination of individual
transactions to determine their nature rather than the
rote learning of numerous possible transactions—began
to emerge. The new abstract approach to accounting
taught students how to apply logic, rather than rules
of thumb and memorised examples, to bookkeeping
problems.

Despite the general theoretical consensus about how
business books should be kept and the dominance of
the double-entry method in bookkeeping literature,
approaches varied enormously in practice and double
entry was not widely used until the rise of the corporation in the nineteenth century, as we shall see. But
if Venetian double entry as codified by Pacioli was not
widely practised until the nineteenth century, why was it
so attractive to all the early writers and teachers?

First, because of Pacioli's detailed instructions on
making a trial balance, which allowed merchants to
check their books for mistakes. The authors of the early
bookkeeping treatises make it clear that they considered

this to be a great virtue of the Italian system. Teacher and author Stephen Monteage wrote in London in 1682: 'This way of accounting which we Treat of, carries with it its own Proof: And here lies the supreme Excellency and Usefulness of this mystery.' And seventy years later, in 1751, commerce expert Malachy Postlethwayt wrote that the trial balance will 'shew you, that this, of all methods, is the most excellent' and praised the 'agreeable satisfaction' of getting a trial balance to balance.

Second, bookkeeping Italian-style appealed to teachers and busy merchants because it was such a methodical and orderly system and the records it kept were so comprehensive. Because of this, double entry became associated with 'good' bookkeeping. This notion of 'good' bookkeeping was soon extended to the point that the use of double entry was seen to confer moral legitimacy on a merchant's work. As Pacioli had, Hugh Oldcastle encouraged merchants to use their account books as a space in which to invoke God. He wrote in 1588: 'it behoveth him [the merchant] first in all his workes and business to call to minde the name of God in all such writings, or in any other reckonings, that he shall beginne'. The first cashbook of the Bank of England, established in 1694, opens with 'Laus Deo'—'Praise God'. As we saw with the merchant of Prato and with Pacioli, such appeals to God were a common feature of the earliest double-entry books and in some parts of Europe continued until the eighteenth century: through the exactitude of their earthly accounting, merchants hoped to gain divine approval in God's heavenly accounts.

Third, the idea of 'good' bookkeeping was later extended to the idea that double-entry bookkeeping was an excellent method for improving the minds of young men, a sort of mental gymnastics, because of the focus and methodical thought it demanded. John Mair, writing in 1765, expresses this view of double entry: 'The theory of this art or science is beautiful and curious, very fit for improving the minds of youth, exercising their wit and invention, and disposing them to a close and accurate way of thinking.' But what of those 'slothful' and 'ignorant' merchants and shopkeepers who failed to use double entry? Nineteenth-century French entrepreneur and jeweller Charles Christofle believed that: 'First, it causes trouble in mind and disquietness of body with hindrance in substance. Secondarily, it is great shame and dishonesty to him that keeps not his book exactly. Thirdly, the evil keeping thereof so vexes the body that it breeds fevers and diseases.' In 1711, English writer and politician Joseph Addison wrote in *The Spectator*: 'This phrase ["he has not kept true Accompts"] bears the highest Reproach; for a Man to be mistaken in the Calculation of his Expense, in his Ability to answer future Demands, or to be impertinently sanguine in putting his Credit to too great Adventure, are all Instances of as much Infamy, as with gayer Nations to be failing in Courage or common Honesty.' This equation of moral rectitude and good accounting was first seen almost two millennia earlier in Cicero and is echoed in Leon Battista Alberti's 1440 observation: 'We shall ever give ground to honour. It will stand to us like a public accountant, just, practical, and prudent in measuring, weighing, considering, evaluating, and assessing everything we do, achieve, think and desire.'

Finally, double entry was praised for its ability to improve decision-making. As Stephen Monteage wrote in 1690:

> Also excellent use might accrue by this
> consideration, that he, who daily sees his
> Accounts fairly and duely kept, knows how
> to steer the Fly-boat of his Expenses, to hoyse
> or lower his Sails of outgoing, according to
> Wisdom: Whereas the ungrounded young
> Merchant reckons at random, goes on and
> sees not the Labyrinth he runs himself into,
> but at haphazard spends prodigally, according
> to his vain surmise on the one side, of Profit
> where little or none is; on the other side, of
> small Expenses where they are thick and
> threefold; and how many are there of these
> everywhere ... that by not seeing or not
> willing to see and set before them the state
> of their Affairs, go on in a secret decaying of
> themselves, to the utter undoing of their poor
> Families!

The profit figures that Pacioli's double entry made it possible to calculate were a vital tool for early merchants, used in their decision-making, forecasting and planning. German business writers Thomas Flugel (1741) and Andreas Wagner (1802) point out that only double entry can show the individual profit figures for each line of merchandise or venture, and it is therefore to be preferred over single entry, which can only show the total profit figure of a business. In his *Accomptant's Oracle* of 1777, Wardhaugh Thompson concurs:

> Book-keeping by Double Entry, or what is commonly called the Italian method of Book-keeping, is the art of keeping our accompts in such a manner, as will not only exhibit to us our neat gain or loss upon each article we deal in, by which we are instructed what branches to pursue, and which to decline; a piece of knowledge so very essential to every man in business, that without it a person can only be said to deal at random, or at best can be called but guess'd work.

By the eighteenth century, double entry had become so pervasive that it had spread beyond the realm of business and into European culture more generally. Daniel Defoe famously applied double-entry bookkeeping in his novel *Robinson Crusoe*, published in 1719. Shipwrecked and alone on the island, Crusoe uses double entry to assess his life, drawing up his 'State of Affairs' and stating 'very impartially, like Debtor and Creditor, the Comforts I'd enjoyed, against the Miseries I suffered', the left-hand side headed 'Evil' and the right-hand side 'Good'. Like the best English shopkeeper, Crusoe keeps account of himself in two columns and 'by this experiment I was made master of my business'. In his manual *The Complete English Tradesman* (1725–27), Defoe addresses bookkeeping more directly, assessing its value to an eighteenth-century merchant. While he is reluctant to attribute to it the powers granted it by some of his contemporaries, nevertheless the phlegmatic Defoe cannot deny bookkeeping's usefulness:

> tho' the exactest book-keeping cannot be
> said to make a tradesman Thrive, or that he
> shall stand the longer in his business, because
> his profit and loss does not depend upon the
> debtors accounts being well posted; yet this
> must be said, that the well keeping of his books
> may be the occasion of his trade being carried
> on with the more ease and pleasure, and
> the more satisfaction, by having numberless
> quarrels, and contentions, and law-suits, which
> are the plagues of a tradesman's life, prevented
> and avoided.

And at the close of the century, Goethe's much-quoted reference to double-entry bookkeeping appeared in his novel *Wilhelm Meister's Apprenticeship*, published in 1795–96. The famous statement about double entry is made by Wilhelm Meister's friend Werner as they debate young Wilhelm's future: the theatre (Wilhelm's choice) or the family business. 'At that time, you had no true idea at all of trade;' says Werner, recalling Wilhelm's childhood when he was smitten by the theatre and spent his days producing theatrical spectaculars with his friends,

> whilst I could not think of any man whose
> spirit was, or needed to be, more enlarged than
> the spirit of a genuine merchant. What a thing
> it is to see the order which prevails throughout
> his business! By means of this he can at
> any time survey the general whole, without
> needing to perplex himself in the details. What
> advantages does he derive from the system of
> book-keeping by double entry? It is among the
> finest inventions of the human mind; every
> prudent master of a house should introduce it
> into his economy.

When Wilhelm questions his friend's view ('you traders commonly, in your additions and balancings, forget what is the proper net-result of life'), Werner once more extols the virtues of trade and bookkeeping:

> My good friend, you do not see how form
> and matter are in this case one; how neither

can exist without the other. Order and
arrangement increase the desire to save and
get. A man embarrassed in his circumstances,
and conducting them imprudently, likes best to
continue in the dark; he will not gladly reckon
up the debtor entries he is charged with. But on
the other hand, there is nothing to a prudent
manager more pleasant than daily to set before
himself the sums of his growing fortune.

Werner echoes sentiments expressed by John Mair
and the other eighteenth-century enthusiasts of double
entry: he believes bookkeeping has an ethical dimension and is the terrain of the morally righteous. Werner
attempts to persuade Wilhelm to choose business over
the theatre because he thinks double-entry bookkeeping will act on him as a moral corrective and a means
to self-improvement. Wilhelm, Goethe's alter ego, is not
persuaded.

Double entry itself is, like any account, a partial and
selective mode of describing aspects of the world. It is
not in itself moral or immoral. Werner's view that it
has a moral dimension is valid only in the context of
the rule of business and commerce, where the proper
conduct of his worldly affairs is the primary concern
of a man's life (women rarely had ownership in this
eighteenth-century commercial realm). The opposing
views of Werner and Wilhelm reflect the beginning of
an antagonism between commerce and art that would

spread through the nineteenth century (Goethe was a major influence on the English Romantic poets) and into the twentieth.

Each and every bookkeeping treatise published on the printing presses of Europe from 1500 to 1800 can be traced back to Pacioli's 1494 *Particularis de computis et scripturis*—and thus Pacioli's 27-page treatise spread Venetian double entry across Europe and thence to America. But three hundred years after its publication, double entry faced its most vehement and controversial challenge. Fittingly, it came from the new economic engine of the industrial age: England.

6

DOUBLE ENTRY MORPHS: THE INDUSTRIAL REVOLUTION AND THE BIRTH OF A PROFESSION

... bookkeeping dozed for several centuries, and
it was not until about four hundred years after
Paciolo's book that a startling awakening took
place ... Why this new prominence in a subject
taught before 1500? The answer is so obvious that
explanation seems impertinent. The end of the
nineteenth, even more than the end of the fifteenth
century, was marked by a most extraordinary
expansion of business.

A.C. LITTLETON, 1933

Indeed, it might be claimed that the joint stock
company was responsible for the transformation of
book-keeping into accounting ...

BASIL YAMEY, 1978

B Y THE END OF THE NINETEENTH CENTURY, PACIOLI'S double-entry bookkeeping had dropped its 'Italian-style' epithet, gone global and morphed into a brand-new profession: accounting. What fired this profound transformation? Essentially, the industrial revolution and the rise of a new form of business organisation, known as the joint stock company. Double entry proved remarkably adaptable to each new demand made upon it by the burgeoning and increasingly complex commercial world. While most medieval practices—such as medicine based on astrological analysis—were found wanting in this industrial age, Venetian bookkeeping came into its own. By 1900, most businesses across the planet, even late adopters like the Rothschild banks, were keeping their books in Pacioli's double entry.

But before double-entry bookkeeping could become entrenched in modern business and spawn a profession, it faced a major theoretical challenge from Europe's new hub of commercial activity.

The attempt to overthrow Pacioli's system was launched in England by Edward Thomas Jones in a book published in 1796 (the same year as Goethe's *Wilhelm Meister's Apprenticeship*) and modestly titled *Jones' English System of Book-keeping by Single or Double Entry, in which it is impossible for an error of the most trifling amount to be passed unnoticed. Calculated effectually to prevent the evils attendant on the methods so long established and adapted to every species of trade.* Jones's book proposed an allegedly infallible new system of bookkeeping by single entry—and it caused a sensation. The passions it inspired and the international furore it provoked are unequalled in the history of bookkeeping and accounting.

Jones opens with an attack on Italian bookkeeping: ' "For every debit there must be a credit, and for every credit there must be a debit"—Alas! How few consider that if this *must* be the case, this the rule to go by, nothing is more easy than to make a set of books wear the appearance of correctness, which at the same time is *full of errors*, or of *false entries*, made on purpose to deceive!' Jones claims that double entry is 'capable of being converted into a cloak for the vilest statements that designing ingenuity can fabricate. A man may defraud his partner, or a book-keeper his employer, if he be so disposed, without ever being detected.' Jones's allegations against double entry are well founded—but, as it turned out, his method for preventing its potential for deception was not.

Jones advertised his own bookkeeping system as labour-saving and mistake-detecting, claiming it would make errors impossible and backing it with testimonials by prominent figures such as MP Robert Peel and the governor of the Bank of England. But in fact his system was no more than a cumbersome, complex version of Pacioli's and has been summarised as follows: instead of two columns in the ledger, make ten; and then in all essential points proceed as directed by Pacioli. Jones and his claims for the labour-saving virtues of his system were so persuasive they almost undid his book's potential success: in an era of rioting provoked by the introduction of labour-replacing machinery such as the power loom and the spinning jenny, the public worried that the purported efficiency of Jones's system—'the most extensively useful invention which had ever made its appearance'—would put bookkeepers out of work. Once Jones had reassured them that no such thing would happen, that no jobs would be lost through the adoption of his system, his book, 'by unblushing impudence', went on to find phenomenal success.

Jones' English System became the first English work on accounting to achieve international fame. It was translated into German, Dutch, Danish, French, Italian and Russian, and an American edition was published in 1797. But unfortunately, Jones's system proved utterly unequal to the task of bookkeeping. This was later confirmed by Jones himself twenty years after its publication, when he abandoned his system in favour of Pacioli's—and thus, as Yamey put it (invoking the religious dimension that so often accompanies double entry), 'the false prophet had become a supporter of the true faith of double entry'.

Despite the failure of Jones's system, its notoriety brought bookkeeping fame and the attention of the general public for the first time, prompted a range of novel double-entry accounting theories, and, ironically, established double entry as the only complete method of recording commercial transactions, thereby cementing it as the foundation of the modern corporate era. Fifty years after Jones's book appeared, Pacioli's double entry had become synonymous with bookkeeping itself. By the end of the nineteenth century there were books on double-entry accounting for factories, stock exchanges, asylums, solicitors, county councils, banks, railways, hotels, restaurants, gold prospectors, electric lighting, brewers, retailers, hospitals, insurance companies and numerous other enterprises.

THE NEW WORLD OF FACTORIES

This vast new range of double-entry applications reflects the extraordinary expansion of business from the late eighteenth century to the close of the nineteenth, a period which saw the rise of the joint stock company (a business organisation which was funded by selling shares to investors who became partners in the venture), and marks the formative era of accountancy. During these decades, accountants transformed a mere system of recording exchanges into a method of managing and controlling business. The first signs that double entry would be equal to the task of monitoring and directing this new industrial world of factories, wage labour and large-scale capital investment were found in the north of England, in the pottery works of Her Majesty's potter, Josiah Wedgwood (1730–95)—a factory called Etruria, named, by chance, after the ancient Italian region home to Pacioli's Sansepolcro.

An entrepreneurial and marketing genius, Wedgwood built the world's first industrialised pottery manufactory. He found his customers among the new upwardly mobile classes whose insatiable wants were described by political economist Nathaniel Forster in 1767: 'the perpetual restless ambition in each of the inferior ranks to raise themselves to the level of those immediately above them', he said, caused fashionable luxury to spread 'like a contagion'. Among the most coveted fashionable luxuries of the day were Wedgwood's vases. So ravenous was the appetite of the cashed-up classes for his vases that Wedgwood described it as a 'violent Vase Madness'. He marvelled at the crush in 1769 in his new London showrooms, where there was 'no getting to the door for Coaches, nor into the rooms for Ladies & Gentlemen . . . Vases was all the cry. We must endeavour to gratify this *universal passion*.' But the mania for Wedgwood vases brought the firm such sudden success that it could not meet demand. By late 1769, Wedgwood and his partner Thomas Bentley had serious cash-flow problems and an accumulation of stock, 'classic symptoms of uncontrolled expansion with insufficient capital resources'.

In response, in 1772 Wedgwood decided to use double-entry bookkeeping to undertake a rigorous and comprehensive examination of his firm's accounts and business practices. The results of his endeavours proved to be enlightening. He found the firm's pricing was haphazard, its production runs too short to be economical, and it was spending unexpectedly large amounts on raw materials, labour and other costs, without collecting its bills fast enough to finance expanding production. During this period of scrutiny, Wedgwood made an important discovery—the distinction between fixed and variable costs—and he immediately understood the implications of their difference for the management of his business. He told Bentley that their greatest costs—modelling and molds, rent, fuel, wages—were fixed: 'Consider that these expences move like clockwork, & are much the same whether the quantity of goods made be large or small.' And because of these fixed costs which remained the same regardless of how much was produced, the more their factory produced, the cheaper these fixed costs would be per unit of production. As Wedgwood pointed out: 'you will see the vast consequence in most manufactures of *making the greatest quantity possible in a given time.*' In other words, by scrutinising his books using double entry in the new industrial world, Wedgwood had uncovered the commercial benefits of mass production.

This is one of the earliest instances of the use of double-entry bookkeeping to analyse business accounts and apply the financial information thus extracted to guide business strategy and decision-making in the new industrial world. Now known as cost accounting, it has become an important branch of management accounting. Wedgwood's examination of his costs was a response to the problems raised by the new industrial business conditions created by the factory system and is an early example of the way in which the industrial revolution transformed double-entry bookkeeping. (The fortune Wedgwood made from his pioneering venture into cost accounting and rigorously managed pottery works was well used: in 1831 it helped to underwrite his grandson Charles Darwin's famous voyage on the *Beagle*.)

The shift in outlook required to move Pacioli's bookkeeping system beyond its mercantile origins in an exchange economy (where it recorded the exchange of goods, owing and being owed, paying and collecting debts) to manufacturing, where the emphasis is on the production of goods (the conversion of materials and labour into products) was huge. Two books on account-keeping for factories published soon after Wedgwood's early forays into cost accounting show the conceptual difficulties posed by the need to incorporate new elements—labour and materials per unit of production—into an enterprise's accounting system so managers could calculate the cost of each unit of production. Both books—*Essai sur la tenue des livres d'un manufacturier* by Jean-Baptiste Payen (France, 1817) and *Double Entry by Single* by F.W. Cronhelm (London, 1818)—attempt to solve the problem of accounting for factory production: tracking the way that labour and materials were converted into a new product which was then sold for cash to pay those who had contributed to its production. Among Payen's examples are a carriage manufacturer who uses two sets of records, one 'in money' for its commercial exchanges, one 'in goods' for its production, in an attempt to resolve the problem; and a glue factory which transferred part of the value of the fixed assets—furnaces, boilers and tools—to the cost of the manufactured product. Of the two pioneering publications, Payen's was the more successful: he almost managed to adapt double-entry bookkeeping to manufacturing accounts. The difficulty lay in the fact that the transactions needed to incorporate the manufacturing of products into the existing double-entry system were not financial transactions; they did not involve the exchange of goods but such manoeuvres as adding the cost of labour acquired or material bought, or transferring the cost of materials from the storehouse accounts to the factory account. These sorts of 'non-financial' transactions were, as Littleton puts it, 'strangers among the kinds of transactions which had been familiar for perhaps 300 years or more. To fit such newcomers into the long established scheme was no easy task; it necessitated a new view of the purposes and possibilities of bookkeeping.'

But after a century of factory production, by the 1880s such accounting problems had been better grasped and writers on the subject had brought the two spheres—commerce and manufacturing—together into one coordinated system of books. E. Garcke and J.M. Fells, the authors of *Factory Accounts* (London, 1887), provided for the first time to English readers 'a systematized statement of the principles regarding factory accounts'. Their double-entry system combined the elements of factory production and of exchange—wages, stock, goods in process, produce in the warehouse, costs, sales, profits—so that the flow of price data through the ledger accounts was concurrent with the corresponding flow of work through the manufacturing processes which converted labour and raw materials into commodities.

RAILWAYS

Not only did a new form of production—factories—challenge and alter double-entry bookkeeping from the 1770s, but the financing and managing of the vast investments required to build railways during the same period of industrial expansion brought new issues of accounting and accountability. The first proper paying passenger railway—the Liverpool and Manchester Railway—opened in Britain in 1830, and from then on railway progress was phenomenal. In just twenty years, 9700 kilometres of track were laid and by 1850 the largest railway company, London and North Western, employed 15,000 people. Nothing on this financial scale had ever been seen before. Most other successful industries of the time—pottery, cotton, wool, iron—had started small and grown through the reinvestment of their own profits. But in the case of railways, this was not possible. Huge amounts of capital expenditure were required at the outset and they were raised not through profits but from private investors on stock exchanges at a 10 per cent dividend, and managed by joint stock companies.

This form of collective investment had been used in Britain from 1600 by enterprises such as the East India Company to finance long and dangerous sea voyages. But a rash of speculation and spectacular losses brought its growth to an abrupt halt with the passing in 1720 of the so-called 'Bubble Act', which prohibited all joint stock companies not authorised by royal charter. When the Bubble Act was eventually repealed in 1825, a second and abiding era of joint stock activity dawned in Britain—and with it came the metamorphosis of book-keeping into a new profession: accounting. Economist Basil Yamey argues that this was accounting's formative moment: 'Indeed, it might be claimed that the joint stock company was responsible for the transformation of book-keeping into accounting and for the profession of accountancy.'

When railway companies faltered in the late 1840s, struggling to return 10 per cent on investments, many began to fiddle their books. For example, they treated costs as capital investments rather than as expenses, thereby inflating their profits; and used fresh investments instead of profits to pay out dividends (a strategy now known as a Ponzi scheme, made infamous most recently by Bernie Madoff in 2009). The most notorious perpetrator of deceptive railway accounting was the 'Railway King', George Hudson (1800–71), who by 1844 controlled over 1600 kilometres of railway in Britain. Hudson overstated his profits and used shareholder investments to pay dividends. When he was eventually exposed by a group of outraged investors, he fled England to escape lawsuits against him for outstanding sums amounting to almost £600,000, a fortune at the time. Ironically, if Hudson and other nineteenth-century railway tycoons had been obliged to comply with today's more comprehensive accounting standards, it is possible the vast railway systems of the nineteenth century would never have been built.

Hudson's and other, similar cases of fraud and corporate failure led to growing pressure on the British government to regulate industry to protect creditors and investors on the new stock markets. Investors called for companies to keep publicly available financial statements based on reliable accounting records. But the existing laissez-faire system suited most British parliamentarians, many of whom had vested corporate interests, including shares in the very railway companies in question. A comment made in 1837 by the president of the Board of Trade, Charles Poulett Thomson, sums up their attitude: 'It is by the Government not meddling with capital that this country has been able to obtain a superiority over every other country.'

REGULATION

~

But the British parliament did eventually intervene to curb the free rein of capital, starting with the Joint Stock Companies Act of 1844, which specified the conditions of company formation and required the disclosure of financial information. Under its rule, companies had to account for capital and distinguish it from income, which was essential if dividends were to be properly paid to shareholders out of profit, and not out of capital. Under the Act, companies had to be publicly registered, present a 'full and fair' balance sheet at the annual shareholders' meeting, pay dividends out of profits, maintain capital, and ensure their accounts were audited by people other than the company directors.

The Companies Act of 1862 was another major landmark for accountants. Historian Richard Brown calls it 'the accountant's friend' because it required the presence of accountants at every phase of a public company: at its formation, during its working life and at its liquidation. In the 42 years after the act was passed, 87,821 companies were registered and 50,534 were dissolved, each requiring accountants every step of the way. Needless to say, the workload of accountants increased exponentially over the nineteenth century, as did their numbers: in 1811 there were 24 accounting firms listed in the London directories; by 1883 there were 840.

General incorporation laws—which allowed corporations to be formed without requiring a special government charter—spread rapidly after this: to France (1867), Germany (1870), Hungary (1875), Italy (1882), Switzerland (1883) and Spain (1885).

The numerous financial crises and economic depressions that plagued Britain during the period from the Napoleonic War at the beginning of the nineteenth century to the American Civil War in 1861–65 also created a demand for accountants. The Bankruptcy Act of 1831—which specified that only 'merchants, bankers, accountants or traders' chosen by the Lord Chancellor should be charged with overseeing bankruptcies—was the first government recognition of the new profession of accounting. And the commercial disasters of 1847–48 which led to the Bankruptcy Act of 1849 further established the profession—or, as one accountant of the time put it: 'did more than anything else to place professional accountancy on a solid and substantial basis'. The earliest English bankruptcy data, from 1817, records 2311 bankruptcies; over the next fifty years that figure had risen almost fivefold, to 10,396 in 1869. In response, seven bankruptcy statutes were passed from 1825 to 1883, all of which specified that only those experienced in accounts could handle a bankrupt's affairs. Some of the twentieth century's biggest accounting firms were established in London during this period: William Deloitte opened his practice in 1845; Samuel Price and Edwin Waterhouse in 1849; and William Cooper in 1854.

Accounting for the corporation

~

An unintended consequence of these statutes was the formation of an increasingly well defined profession of accounting. In 1800, financial statements were an incidental product of an enterprise's bookkeeping system and there was no set of generally applied accounting conventions. By 1900 and increasingly thereafter, annual financial statements had become the raison d'être of bookkeeping systems. Fifteenth-century Venetian bookkeeping (which had its roots in the thirteenth century) proved to be the perfect mechanism for generating these financial statements and thus well able to meet the new demands of the corporate era. As Littleton said in 1933: 'The elasticity of bookkeeping as an instrumentality of record still astonishes us 130 years later, for it is still able to shoulder added responsibilities.'

The key accounting issue in a corporation is the amount of profit available for dividends—which means that a corporation must properly distinguish between capital and income, because profits derive from income, not from capital. This new laser-like focus on profits and dividends brought two new accounting questions to centre stage: How to calculate income or profit? And how to value assets? These questions were rarely asked before 1850 but by the end of the century they had become the major preoccupations of practising accountants.

Remarkably, the answer to the first question was found in Pacioli's double entry, a tool perfectly made for distinguishing between capital and income and therefore for calculating profit. The power of calculating the difference between capital and income is one of the basic characteristics of double-entry bookkeeping, and the need to make this distinction in order to calculate dividends became one driving force behind the international adoption of double-entry bookkeeping. Or, as Littleton put it, 'Italian double-entry bookkeeping, already well developed and in a sense awaiting its destiny' provided the mechanism for separating capital and income, and therefore for calculating profit, 'under most diverse and, as future generations were to demonstrate, unexpected circumstances'.

The concept of 'limited liability'—which protected investors from the losses incurred by the organisations in which they had invested—was another accounting issue raised by the joint stock company. Limited liability soon became a legally required characteristic of the corporation and made the distinction between capital and income a legal necessity. It was specifically allowed for in France in the Commercial Code of 1807, and in Scotland and Ireland around the same time. But it did not exist in England. As one English Lord put it in 1788, 'the law of England is otherwise, the rule being that if a partner shares in the advantages, he also shares in all disadvantages'. Because of its traumatic first experiences of joint stock companies, early British corporate law provided for the *unlimited* liability of associates. (That is, investors were liable for the debts and losses of the businesses they had invested in.) Only in 1855, under the Limited Liability Act, were British companies registered under the Joint Stock Companies Act of 1844 allowed to obtain certificates of limited liability; and only in 1862 did the new Companies Act provide generally for the limited liability of corporations.

The advent of the corporation raised several other key accounting issues; for example, how to calculate the declining values—due to wear and tear—of large investments in machinery, rails, rolling stock (or railway vehicles), and so on. This problem gave rise to the concept of depreciation. And how were companies to assign expenses and revenues in this new corporate continuum where there is no obvious end to a business cycle, where 'no ship arrives to signal that it is time to balance accounts and calculate profits'? With the ongoing life of a corporation, there is no 'natural' business period, as there was in the Middle Ages; for example, the length of a ship's voyage. Artificial and arbitrary accounting periods had to be created—such as our accounting period of a year—so managers could allocate expenses and revenues consistently to work out how much each item had cost to produce and how much it had earned (which was essential if profit was to be calculated and dividends determined).

In short, much of what we take for granted in today's corporate machinery evolved in fits and starts with the emergence and regulation of joint stock companies in

Victorian Britain: the idea of a corporation as a legal entity; the idea that a corporation is an ongoing concern which yields an income as 'dividends'—that it is not a series of separate, self-contained speculative ventures with profits and losses paid out as 'divisions' of capital at the end of each new venture as had been the case, for example, among the merchants of Venice; the idea of limited liability; the concept of depreciation; the practice of cost accounting; and the formal establishment of auditing.

Auditing had a long history in England, dating back to as early as 1311, when the records of the chamberlains of the City of London were required to be audited—or 'heard', because at the time very few people could read and even fewer could write (hence 'audit', from the Latin for 'to hear'). In the sixteenth century it was still customary to 'hear' the accounts, but by the seventeenth century written records and documentary evidence were increasingly required. The Joint Stock Companies Act of 1844 and the Companies Clauses Consolidation Act of 1845 made auditing one of accountants' new and primary responsibilities. The role of the auditor was consolidated in Britain with the Companies Act of 1900, which mandated compulsory and uniform annual audits for all registered companies. With the advent of compulsory auditing, accountants became ubiquitous and their professional status in the community rose.

A NEW PROFESSION

~

The mood in the courts and parliament towards the new profession, however, was hostile. 'The whole affairs in bankruptcy have been handed over to an ignorant set of men called accountants, which was one of the greatest abuses ever introduced into the law,' said a British judge from the bench in 1875. The Lord Chancellor, Henry Brougham, held a similarly disdainful view, describing accountants as those who 'could give no proper account of themselves'. Brougham's comment reflects the rapid increase from around 1800 in the number of people in England who called themselves accountants without having any particular expertise in the field and who gave the nascent profession a bad name. And so it is not surprising to find that as the century wore on a number of legitimate, experienced practitioners decided to distinguish themselves from the herd. In the 1870s, a group of accountants rallied together to apply for a charter so they could form a professional association with restricted membership, thereby distinguishing themselves from the charlatans in their midst and elevating their status to that of other professionals such as lawyers and doctors.

The precedent for accounting's professional organisation had been set two decades earlier in Scotland, where accountants were held in unusually high regard, as Scottish poet and novelist Sir Walter Scott made clear in a letter to his brother in 1820: 'If my nephew is steady, cautious, fond of a sedentary life and quiet pursuits, and at the same time a proficient in arithmetic, and with a disposition towards the prosecution of its highest branches, he cannot follow a better line than that of an accountant. It is highly respectable.' Another Scotsman, the Edinburgh accountant Robert Balfour, had this to say in defence of his profession when tempted by a friend to abandon his work for the law:

> It is certainly more varied than that of the
> lawyer, and I believe it to be certainly not less
> dignified. It embraces the extensive field of
> insurance, which has occupied the attention
> of many of the profoundest thinkers that
> Europe has produced, and which, even yet,
> is in its infancy; banking, which regulates
> the prosperity of nations and influences the
> civilisation of the world; finance, whether
> it be the bankruptcy of a nation or, what is
> often just as difficult to manage, of a private
> individual, and then, on the other hand, there
> are arbitrations where conflicting parties,
> placing unlimited confidence in the caution
> and sagacity of the accountant, voluntarily
> entrust him with the arrangements of their
> disputes. And then . . . there are the details of
> general business in which most of us to some
> extent engage. It is here that the profession
> is little more than an infant one, and that no

measures have been taken for reducing it to a
proper shape. This can and ought to be done.

In 1854, the Society of Accountants in Edinburgh
was incorporated by royal charter to regulate professional conduct and provide entry examinations for
those wishing to practise accounting, thus creating
the title 'Chartered Accountant'. In their petition to
Queen Victoria requesting its formation, the Edinburgh
accountants made the following case for the importance
and high standing of their practice:

> that the profession of Accountants, to which
> the Petitioners belong, is of long standing
> and great respectability, and has of late years
> grown into very considerable importance: That
> the business of Accountant, as practised in
> Edinburgh, is varied and extensive, embracing
> all matters of account, and requiring for
> its proper execution not merely a thorough
> knowledge of those departments of business
> which fall within the province of the Actuary,
> but an intimate acquaintance with the
> general principles of law, particularly the law
> of Scotland, and more especially with those
> branches of it which have relation to the Law
> Merchant, to insolvency and bankruptcy, and
> to all rights connected with property.

Some years later, in March 1880, several British accounting societies were incorporated by royal charter into the Institute of Chartered Accountants in England and Wales (ICAEW). The new institute chose the prominent architect John Belcher to design the hall for its new headquarters in Moorgate, London, which were completed in 1890. Belcher's grand Baroque design—one of the first neo-Baroque buildings in London—borrowed from the buildings of more established professions such as medicine and the law, giving the fledgling profession an aura of gravitas and permanence, while its site near banks, gentlemen's clubs and the buildings of Sir Christopher Wren lent it dignity by association.

Similar accounting societies soon spread throughout the British Empire, the first being established in Canada in 1880. The Antipodes took to the new profession with astonishing enthusiasm. By 1899 six institutes of accountants had been established in Australia. In 1905 in Australia and New Zealand there was one chartered accountant for every 4000 people, a striking figure when compared to Scotland's one accountant for 6500 people, Italy's one for 13,000, and England and Wales' one for 10,500. By this time there were about 11,000 accountants enrolled in societies around the world.

By 1900 there were professional accounting associations in much of Europe—Germany, Italy, Holland, Sweden, Belgium—but there were no professional accountants in Portugal, Greece, Finland, Poland and Bulgaria. In Russia there were no public accountants, only bookkeepers, and Russian merchants continued to conduct their business using an abacus, without proper account books, and therefore with few written records. In Tolstoy's *Anna Karenina*, set in 1870s Russia, the hero and landowner Levin seems to relish this arrangement among Russian farmers, which preserves a sense of the sacred calling of tending the earth and keeps farming from becoming just one more commercial activity. He muses about the ancient ways which still prevail in Russian farming and are so unlike the 'Italian bookkeeping' which is taking over Europe: 'Yes, it's a strange thing . . . The way we live like this without reckoning, as if we've been appointed, like ancient vestals, to tend some sort of fire.'

Through Levin, Tolstoy expresses his general unease with the encroaching 'rationalisation' of life—the measurement of time and space of which double entry was a part—brought by science, accounting and the new forms of production that spread across Europe in the nineteenth century. He was just one of many writers and artists who were deeply suspicious of such modernisation. The English Romantic poets took a similar view—vividly captured in William Blake's 'satanic mills'—as did Dostoyevsky, who in *The Idiot* writes of ' "the whole spirit of the last few centuries, taken as a whole, sir, in its scientific and practical application, is perhaps really damned, sir!" ' In the twentieth century, writers such as E.M. Forster and D.H. Lawrence equally damned the new scientific and commercial spirit that tore people from the earth. Only now, many decades on, are their warnings against the dangers inherent in this new worldview becoming obvious to us in the form of an environmental crisis.

THE NEW COMMERCIAL POWERHOUSE

Things were somewhat different in America, where the corporation was as energetically encouraged as a symbol of initiative and freedom as it was initially suspected in Britain as a source of chaos and ruin. Once the American colonies had thrown off British law, starting in 1775, various states passed statutes relating to corporations. The first incorporation laws, for ecclesiastical, educational or literary associations, were introduced in South Carolina in 1778 and in New York in 1784. The New York Stock Exchange opened in 1792 and by 1827 it was trading the stocks of twelve banks, nineteen insurance companies and the New York Light Company, the first public utility in America. In 1795 the first statute for freely incorporating business enterprises was passed in North Carolina, for canal construction: 'Here for the first time since the beginning of the Roman Empire, a sovereign state offered incorporation for business purposes to any who desired it, freely and on equal terms.' In 1811 a New York statute allowed the incorporation of manufacturing companies, and in Michigan in 1837 the principle was extended to banking. As in Britain, the capital needed to build and operate the canals and railways was raised by corporations on stock exchanges, and by 1850, cash statements, balance sheets and sometimes income statements were provided for investors.

With its vast resources, entrepreneurial spirit and large domestic market, and a commercial culture characterised by incorporation, continual measurement and managerial accounting, over the course of the nineteenth century the United States overtook Europe to become by 1900 the world's largest economy. Fortunes were made by steel entrepreneur Andrew Carnegie, gunpowder manufacturer Irénée du Pont, oil magnate John D. Rockefeller and financier John Pierpont Morgan, all of whom used cost accounting techniques to manage their business empires. Rockefeller started out as a bookkeeper and attributed his vast wealth and the success of his company, Standard Oil, to his mastery of double-entry bookkeeping, especially cost accounting.

The Institute of Accountants and Bookkeepers of New York (IABNY) was formed in 1882 and the American Association of Public Accountants (AAPA)—a national body under the sway of the British Chartered Accountants—was incorporated in 1887. Broadly speaking, US and British accountants had opposing views of their profession, particularly regarding the question of whether accounting was an art or a science: American-born accountants considered accountancy to be a science, while their British counterparts—and the American members of AAPA who followed them—favoured common sense and practical wisdom, stressing 'the virtue, experience and steady judgement of the seasoned accountant'.

The American scientific approach was developed on the factory floor by engineers, who used job analysis and time-and-motion studies to work out 'scientific' standards for the quantities of materials and labour required to produce each unit of output. To compete with the more successful British-style 'Chartered Accountants', in 1896 the IABNY granted the title 'Certified Public Accountant' (CPA) to its members, and required a university education for anyone who wanted the title of CPA. The United States thus became the first jurisdiction to specify a university degree for accountants and to provide tertiary courses in accounting, such as those at the School of Commerce, Accounts and Finance connected with the University of New York. In at least two US universities—the University of Birmingham and the New York University School of Commerce—the tertiary teaching of accounting had become so well established by 1905 that it had been elevated to a professor's chair.

In 1914 Professor John B. Geijsbeek published the first English translation of Luca Pacioli's bookkeeping treatise in the United States—*Ancient Double-Entry Bookkeeping: Luca Pacioli's treatise*—for his students and for all American accountants, believing that 'they who wish to obtain knowledge of any science must first learn its history and then trace its gradual growth'.

Geijsbeek wanted to give 'an added assurance' to those who believed accountancy was a science that they were correct in their belief, 'that the apparently empirical rules of commerce are based upon an ancient scientific and mathematical foundation'—that is, upon Pacioli's *De computis*.

The study and status of accounting received a further boost in the United States in 1933, when accounting professor A.C. Littleton published a book on the history of the subject from Pacioli to 1900. He asks whether accounting, 'the late claimant for recognition as a profession', is entitled to some respect in the professional sphere or must 'consort with crystal gazing, chiropractice and palm reading'. His reply—affirming that accounting can claim respect as a profession—is based on the continuing relevance and veracity of Fra Luca Pacioli's 1494 treatise:

> Let those who vaunt the superior merits of
> other disciplines remember that this first
> presentation made by Paciolo was not crude
> and incorrect, but contained the essentials
> of bookkeeping as we know it today, despite
> the fact that it was written at a time when
> chemistry partook of the vagaries of alchemy,
> biology was a weird collection of errors, and
> medicine had more in common with the
> medicine man than it has even today.

Littleton wrote his book to remove the 'stigma attached to accounting' in the eyes of other, older professions by showing that its origins—Pacioli's treatise—are impeccable and that it has attracted serious thinkers, those 'of unquestioned intellectual attainment'. And further, to demonstrate that accounting is a vocation with the soundest of purposes: it 'justifies itself in that it has arisen to meet a social need, for its function is to place responsibility, to prevent fraud, to guide industry, to determine equities, to solve the all essential conundrum of business: "What are my profits?"' Thus the accounting profession established itself on the firm foundations of Pacioli's 1494 *De computis*.

And so from the mercantile capitalism of Pacioli's fifteenth century to the increasingly complex industrial capitalism of the nineteenth, nearly all the demands made for accounting information could be met within a single framework: double entry. It could accurately record business transactions, it could distinguish between capital and income as required by nineteenth-century law and investors, it could distinguish between private expenses and corporate costs, and it could produce data that helped to evaluate past investment decisions. By 1900, Pacioli's Venetian bookkeeping had morphed into a flourishing profession whose services were essential— and required by law—for the functioning of a new era: the age of the corporation.

At the beginning of this new century, a German economist would contend that double entry was not merely a tool of business, but the catalyst of an entire economic system, one that had only recently been named and was being increasingly theorised: capitalism.

7

DOUBLE ENTRY AND CAPITALISM—CHICKEN AND EGG?

It is simply impossible to imagine capitalism
without double-entry bookkeeping; they are like
form and content.

WERNER SOMBART, *DER MODERNE KAPITALISMUS*, 1902

Above all, Luca [Pacioli] laid the foundation of
the modern conception of profit, not as some
vague increase in possession, as in antiquity, but as
something hard, even crystalline, mathematical and
open to empirical test at any time whatever through
an interlocking system of books.

JAMES BUCHAN, 1997

IN 1902 A MOST INTRIGUING CLAIM WAS MADE ON behalf of double entry. It was proposed by a German economist, Werner Sombart (1863–1941), in his six-volume work on capitalism, *Der moderne Kapitalismus*. In six pages Sombart set out his belief that the emergence of capitalism and the appearance of double-entry book-keeping in the thirteenth century are causally related. He wrote: 'It is simply impossible to imagine capitalism without double-entry bookkeeping; they are like form and content.' In Sombart's view, capitalism and double entry are so intimately connected it is difficult to tell which was cause and which effect: 'one may indeed doubt whether capitalism has procured in double-entry book-keeping a tool which activates its forces, or whether double-entry book-keeping has first given rise to capitalism out of its own spirit.'

Sombart defines capitalism as

> a particular economic system, recognisable as
> an organisation of trade, consisting invariably
> of two collaborating sections of the population,
> the owners of the means of production, who
> also manage them, and property-less workers,
> bound to the markets which they serve; which
> displays the two dominant principles of wealth
> creation and economic rationalism.

Sombart's definition derives from Karl Marx. Friedrich Engels, Marx's collaborator and editor, wrote of Sombart's work: 'It is the first time that a German professor succeeds on the whole in seeing in Marx's writings what Marx really says.'

In 1902, the word 'capitalism' had only recently been coined. It is said to have first appeared in 1850, in

French politician and historian Louis Blanc's *Organisation du travail*, where Blanc used it to make the following distinction: 'This sophism consists of perpetually confusing the usefulness of capital with what I shall call capitalism, in other words the appropriation of capital by some to the exclusion of others. Let everyone shout "Long live capital". We shall applaud and our attack on capitalism, its deadly enemy, shall be all the stronger.' The word was, however, rarely used during the nineteenth century, even by Marx.

The base word 'capital' evolved from *capitale*, a late Latin word derived from *caput*, meaning 'chief' or 'head', and 'property'. By the end of the thirteenth century, 'capital' was used in bookkeeping to describe the productive wealth of the proprietor—the capital assets of a firm. As we have seen, the calculation of capital is central to the double-entry system; from the capital account, says Pacioli, 'you may always learn what your fortune is'.

It is likely that the concept of capitalism also came from double-entry bookkeeping. French sociologist Eve Chiapello argues that social scientists must have consulted nineteenth-century account books when conceiving the idea of capitalism, because its definition is so intimately tied to the categories and practices of double entry.

One of the first to tap the theoretical possibilities of the language and concepts of double-entry bookkeeping was Karl Marx, who had a special and little-known interest in the bookkeeping activities of nineteenth-century Britain. According to Chiapello, Marx could not have defined capital in the way he does without referring to the accounting practices of his day, because his representation of capital corresponds in every way to its use in nineteenth-century double-entry bookkeeping. If she is right—and her argument is persuasive—then the double-entry bookkeeping practices of industrial Britain made a significant contribution to Marx's definition of capital and therefore to Sombart's definition of capitalism. Which would mean that the very concept of capitalism encapsulates the double-entry system and could not have come into being without it.

But from where did Marx get his knowledge of double entry? How did he access the ledgers of British manufacturing? His extensive correspondence with Engels reveals Marx's fascination with the details of the double-entry accounting practices of the Engels family's cotton mill in England, a major nineteenth-century centre for textile production. Marx writes to Engels: 'If it can be done very briefly, without giving you too much trouble, I would like to have an example of Italian bookkeeping with explanations.' In another letter, dated 4 March 1858, Marx asks: 'how do you calculate capital turnover in your books? The theoretical laws on the matter are simple and self-evident but it is still good to have some idea of how things are presented in practice.' Although Marx said very little about accounting in his published work, he considered bookkeeping to be 'the control and ideal synthesis' of the production process, a control that becomes more necessary the larger and more complex the production process becomes—the more production 'assumes a social scale and loses its purely individual character', as with the factories of industrial Britain. For Marx, accounting was the symbolic reflection in imagination of 'the movement of production, especially of the production of surplus value'.

Engels was in a good position to supply Marx with detailed information about the accounting practices of his family cotton mill. For twenty years from 1850, Engels worked as a clerk in that very same cotton mill, located at the teeming centre of Britain's cotton manufacturing industry, Manchester, where business practices were among the most sophisticated in the world. Engels found the work 'repugnant' but he took it on and persisted with it for two decades, mostly in order to support Marx (and Marx's family) during his long years in the British Library in London researching *Das Kapital*. In fact, British factories guided by Venetian double-entry bookkeeping directly funded two of the great revolutionary thinkers of the nineteenth century: Charles Darwin (through his grandfather Josiah Wedgwood's Etruria pottery works), and Karl Marx through the Engels' cotton mills of Manchester.

As mentioned, Sombart derived his understanding of capital from Marx and developed his theory of the historical link between capitalism and double entry by looking at the evolution of accounting. In his view, this had five stages. The first three stages were the appearance of account books in thirteenth-century Italy, the development of double-entry bookkeeping from around 1350, and the introduction of the capital account and the profit and loss account in around 1430. According to Sombart this third stage, immortalised by Luca Pacioli in 1494, is 'the very essence of double entry bookkeeping' and 'can without a doubt be summed up in this objective: keeping track of every movement throughout the company's capital cycle, quantifying it and recording it in writing'. Sombart calls Pacioli's treatise 'the first scientific system for double-entry bookkeeping in which all previous empirical discoveries were theorized into a coherent, comprehensive representation'. The last two stages of bookkeeping's development came with the publication of Simon Stevin's accounting book in 1605 and the introduction of stocktaking in closing procedures.

According to Sombart, capitalism originated with double-entry bookkeeping, which created the category of capital—or 'that amount of wealth which is used in making profits and which enters into the accounts'. Not content merely with assigning double entry a foundational role in the capitalist economy, Sombart also accords bookkeeping the same parentage as modern science, arguing that 'double-entry bookkeeping was born of the same spirit as the systems of Galileo and Newton, and the modern schools of physics and chemistry'. In fact, he goes further still, suggesting that double entry itself was the germ of the scientific revolution of the sixteenth century: 'Without looking too closely one might already glimpse in double-entry bookkeeping the ideas of gravitation, the circulation of blood and energy conservation.' What Sombart means by this extravagant claim is that through its encouragement of regular record-keeping, mathematical order and the reduction of events to numbers abstracted from time and place, double entry fostered a new view of the world as being subject to quantification—and it was this urge to abstract and quantify natural phenomena that lay at the heart of the scientific revolution. Oswald Spengler makes a similar claim in *The Decline of the West*, where he equates Pacioli with Copernicus.

When we put together all the claims Sombart made on behalf of double-entry bookkeeping, we see that he is effectively arguing that it gave birth to the entire modern scientific capitalist world. In particular, he says that by enabling a numerical, monetary (and hence, in his view, 'rational') calculation of profit, double-entry bookkeeping provided the basis on which commerce could be seen as a process of acquisition: as an unending, systematic pursuit of profit. This claim might seem self-evident in light of this book's view of history through the lens of bookkeeping, but Sombart's contentions are controversial and much contested by economists and historians, as we shall see.

If Sombart's analysis is right and double-entry bookkeeping made possible the explicit pursuit of profit and the accumulation of wealth by merchants, then this would help to explain why the cities of northern Italy, where double-entry bookkeeping first appeared in Europe, amassed such stupendous riches in the fourteenth and fifteenth centuries. The fact that their rulers—the Medici of Florence, Ludovico Sforza of Milan, the doges of Venice, the dukes of Urbino, the governors of Sansepolcro—expended vast sums of this wealth to finance the splendour of their courts, civic buildings and cathedrals makes it possible to argue, as some have, that this Italian accounting innovation produced the Renaissance. As Professor Michael Olmert puts it,

> It was the perfection of accounting in the
> thirteenth century—and specifically the
> invention of double-entry bookkeeping—that
> made Italy great. People from all over Europe
> came to northern Italy to learn the new
> method, which was based on the principle that
> every transaction be recorded twice, as a debit
> and a credit . . . In the end, the Renaissance
> still shapes up as the product of immense
> genius, but genius animated by money and
> the skills essential to commerce.

Another German thinker who argued that double-entry bookkeeping played a key role in history was Sombart's contemporary, the lawyer, political economist and sociologist Max Weber (1864–1920). Although he does not go as far as Sombart, Weber gave double entry a central place in his theory of capitalism, equating capitalism with the development of the capital account in the sixteenth century, a refinement he attributes to Simon Stevin. In his 1904 book *The Protestant Ethic and the Spirit of Capitalism*, Weber distinguishes capitalism from other economic systems partly on the basis of its use of double-entry bookkeeping. He sums up his position in the following way: 'The most general presupposition for the existence of this present-day capitalism is that of rational capital accounting as the norm for all large industrial undertakings which are concerned with provision of everyday wants.'

Weber's definition of a 'capitalistic enterprise' is derived from the concepts of double-entry bookkeeping: 'a rational capitalistic establishment is one with capital accounting'. Like Sombart, Weber argues that double entry is significant because it makes possible an abstract measure of income and expenses—and therefore enables the calculation of profit, the key component of capitalistic business practice. Weber also believed that the formal rationality of double entry made the world a cold and disenchanted place—and, ominously, predicted that double entry would continue its rule 'perhaps until the last ton of fossilized coal is burnt'.

The economist Joseph Schumpeter (1883–1950) also traces the development of capitalism back to double-entry bookkeeping. In *Capitalism, Socialism and Democracy*, published in 1942, Schumpeter says that capitalism adds a new edge to rationality by 'exalting the monetary unit—not itself a creation of capitalism—into a unit of account. That is to say, capitalist practice turns the unit of money into a tool of rational cost-profit calculations, of which the towering monument is double-entry book-keeping.' In his view, double entry's 'cost-profit calculus' drives capitalist enterprise—and then spreads throughout the whole culture: 'And thus defined and quantified for the economic sector, this type of logic or attitude or method then starts upon its conqueror's career subjugating—rationalizing—man's tools and philosophies, his medical practice, his picture of the cosmos, his outlook on life, everything in fact including his concepts of beauty and justice and his spiritual ambitions.' For Schumpeter, capitalism 'generates a formal spirit of critique where the good, the true and the beautiful no longer are honoured; only the useful remains—and that is determined solely by the critical spirit of the account-ant's cost-benefit calculation'.

It is easy to understand the appeal of Sombart's argument, especially in light of the historical coincidence of the rise in thirteenth-century Italy of mercantile capitalism alongside double-entry bookkeeping. But detractors argue that a close reading of the historical evidence does not support Sombart's generalisation: in fact the few merchants' books which survive from the 1300s to 1800 indicate the double-entry system was not then widely adopted in practice. As part of his career-long dispute with Sombart, economist Basil Yamey argues that the spirit of capitalism animated numerous prominent Italian mercantile ventures *before* they adopted Venetian bookkeeping: 'Perhaps it is sufficient to note that the Italian enterprises of the Bardi, Peruzzi, Alberti and Medici cannot be said to have been run less efficiently and "capitalistically" before they had adopted the double-entry system than after they had done so.'

In defence of Sombart, however, Eve Chiapello responds to his critics by suggesting that the links between capitalism and accounting are not so much historical as conceptual, that capitalism could only 'be born conceptually' thanks to double entry—which makes sense of the fact that the only historical links between accounting and capitalism that are outlined by Sombart and also affirmed by historians occur from the second half of the eighteenth century until the end of the nineteenth. It was during this period that the social science of political economy was born, that the work of Adam Smith, Thomas Malthus and David Ricardo was published (and influenced Marx's thinking during the same era). The emerging social sciences looked to accounting for their foundations. It was double entry that allowed economists to build the models they used to analyse economies and revealed to Marx the building blocks of nineteenth-century industrial production and management. And it was Sombart who took up Marx's analysis and used it to develop the concept of 'capitalism', a term he popularised in *Der moderne Kapitalismus*. Only then, at the beginning of the twentieth century, did the word 'capitalism' catch on in intellectual and political spheres and become the natural antonym of socialism.

Despite its dismissal by many historians, the influence of Sombart's thesis has been profound and widespread. In an essay published in 1985, the historian James Aho linked double-entry bookkeeping to the ancient art of rhetoric, the rules used to make persuasive arguments perfected by the Roman lawyer and orator Cicero (an art, incidentally, which Aristotle says sprang from a property dispute). According to this argument, medieval merchants used double-entry bookkeeping as a rhetorical tool of capitalist propaganda, to persuade their 'audience' that their business was honest, morally sound and its profit-making ethically justified.

Why would bookkeeping need to persuade? Because, says Aho, it was used to defend these profit-making businesses against the Church's ban on usury. The rhetoric of a well-kept ledger argued for the honesty of a business and the legitimacy of its profits, as this advice from 1683 makes clear: 'If [the merchant] be fortunate and acquire much, [double entry] directs him the way to Imploy it to the best advantage, if he be unfortunate it satisfies the world of his just dealing, and is the fairest and best Apologie of his Innocence and honesty to the World.' By demonstrating the moral legitimacy of business and profits, double-entry bookkeeping 'provided the apology for the rational pursuit of wealth *par excellence*'.

In a 1991 paper on accounting and rhetoric, Bruce G. Carruthers and Wendy Nelson Espeland argue that the symbolic language of double-entry bookkeeping is as significant as its technical capabilities, a possibility not considered by Sombart and Weber. They argue that a double-entry account is not just a piece of neutral information, but also an 'account' or story; that accounting is not merely a technical practice, but also a means of framing a set of business transactions with a rhetorical purpose. Bookkeeping is a way of making sense of business for an 'audience' that has grown and changed from Pacioli's day to our own.

For example, Carruthers and Espeland argue that the rhetorical agenda of Pacioli's treatise was to convince his readers that Venetian bookkeeping was better than all other methods and to persuade them that business in particular and commerce in general were legitimate pursuits. The issues that Pacioli had to address in his treatise, such as the Church's ban on usury, are no longer relevant today, but accounting still serves a rhetorical purpose. The accounts it generates are still designed to convince an audience of something: for example, of a business's solidity, as we saw with the Royal Bank of Scotland, or of its ongoing success, as in the case of Enron.

In a 2000 essay on biomedical ethics, sociologist John H. Evans discusses why the use of a small set of principles—those of respect for persons, beneficence and justice, first spelled out in the landmark US public health policy paper the *Belmont Report* (1979)—has become common in bioethics today. Evans is interested in the rationale behind the use of a small set of principles to guide decisions (often called 'principlism'), a rationale whose origins have been sought in historical events such as the Nuremberg trials which followed the Second World War. But Evans argues that the rationale behind principlism goes back further, to 1494 and Pacioli's *De computis*. He calls Pacioli's treatise on double-entry bookkeeping 'a major innovation in economic history'. First, because double entry provided the means of discarding all information extraneous to decision-making, leaving behind only numbers. And second, because it translated these numbers into a common measuring tool called 'profit', which allowed a relatively precise evaluation of actions. Double entry thus transformed business books from mere memory aids into records which allow the calculation of profit—and which can therefore be used to measure the success of each individual transaction and of a business generally.

For Evans, double-entry bookkeeping has made possible the cost-benefit thinking that plagues contemporary management, from government and corporations to health care and education. For example, it governs 'the tabulation that any academic department chair is familiar with: what are our costs for the next year, and what is our income? And, more specifically, are the costs associated with this component of the business generating returns that justify the costs?' Like Weber, Evans sees double-entry bookkeeping as key to this particular form of organisation and rationale because it allows us to compare an enterprise's total assets at the beginning of a profit-making venture with the total assets at the end— and thereby to value and determine the potential success (purely in terms of profit) of any potentially profit-making activity, even when non-calculable goods are at stake, such as education and the natural environment.

We are now so familiar with this once innovative (and largely arbitrary) cost-benefit way of thinking that we take it for granted and cannot imagine it otherwise. And yet, as we shall see, this profit-driven way of thinking encouraged by double entry is not only driving managers to drink, academics to pull their hair out, politicians to short-term opportunism and most human beings to suffer in some way, but it is also destroying the world beneath our feet.

And yet the advance of the protean double-entry method continued. From its conquest of corporations and its infiltration of the social sciences, in the mid twentieth century double entry extended its sphere of influence into the accounts of nations.

8

JOHN MAYNARD KEYNES, DOUBLE ENTRY AND THE WEALTH OF NATIONS

Keynes was the first economist to visualize
the economy as an aggregate quantity of
output resulting from an aggregate stream of
expenditure . . . Thus Keynes's aggregate concepts
led directly to the development of national income
accounts . . .

ROBERT SKIDELSKY

[The double-entry bookkeeping approach is] the
hallmark of the national income and product
accounts.

KATHARINE G. ABRAHAM AND CHRISTOPHER MACKIE

WITH THE CRASH OF THE NEW YORK STOCK
Exchange in October 1929 the laissez-faire principles that had guided government approaches to national
economic affairs in the nineteenth century suddenly lost
their lustre. Over the next four years in the United States,

11,000 banks failed, production collapsed by more than a half and unemployment soared, peaking at 13 million or nearly one-quarter of the workforce. At sea in their attempts to develop a coherent response to the crisis, the administrations of Herbert Hoover and then Franklin Delano Roosevelt commissioned Russian-born economist Simon Kuznets to develop comprehensive estimates of the income of the United States to guide their policies. In March 1933, Roosevelt succeeded Hoover as US president and immediately implemented his 'Hundred Days': 'a presidential barrage of ideas and programmes unlike anything known to American history'. The following year, in May 1934, the British economist John Maynard Keynes went to America to see the New Deal in action. In Washington he said: 'Here, not in Moscow, is the economic laboratory of the world.'

The arrival of the British economist in the 'economic laboratory of the world' of 1934 signified a momentous change in both economic theory and government practice, prompted by the Great Depression. Roosevelt's response to the Depression was the New Deal, the first full-scale, systematic government intervention in a capitalist market economy. Keynes's response was to develop a revolutionary theory of market capitalism, his 'theory of effective demand', which he would publish in February 1936 as *The General Theory of Employment, Interest and Money*. The *General Theory* would become enormously influential because it provided a theoretical basis for the measurement of national income, consumption, investment and savings—at the same time as the first moves towards their calculation were being made in Washington. As his biographer Robert Skidelsky says: 'Keynes was the first economist to visualize the economy as an aggregate quantity of output resulting from an aggregate stream of expenditure. This new way of seeing the architecture of an economy is the General Theory's most enduring legacy.'

At the core of both Roosevelt's and Keynes's thinking was an understanding that the unfettered capitalist market economy was prone to collapse and that some form of government intervention was required periodically to resurrect it. Much as the crisis in the Etruria pottery works had led Josiah Wedgwood to examine his books and make the first experiments in cost accounting and account-determined intervention in the workings of a firm, so the economic crisis of the 1930s led Roosevelt and Keynes to devise account books for their nations in order to formulate policies for government intervention in the workings of their economies. As Keynes noted, in the midst of the Depression social experiments were in fashion—and all of them conceived a larger role for government and a greatly restricted role for free commerce.

So how do these twentieth-century capitalist revolutions relate to Luca Pacioli and Venetian double-entry bookkeeping? Both Roosevelt's programme of economic intervention and Keynes's theory of effective demand entailed the construction of national accounting systems: both were concerned with accounting for nations.

And Keynes, the first to offer a systematic way of thinking about the behaviour of an entire economy, applied the principles of double-entry bookkeeping to construct his whole-economy framework. The *General Theory* rests on an understanding that the aggregate output (or real income, 'Y') of an economy is determined by consumption and investment ($Y = C + I$).

When considering the Depression, Keynes theorised that if it were possible to measure in money what the community was buying and how much extra the unemployed would produce if they were working, then it would be possible to calculate how much extra 'demand' (or spending) would need to be injected into the economy to close this 'output gap' (created by the unemployed). In other words, it would be possible to determine how much the government itself would have to spend in order for the economy to reach full employment. Keynes's framework introduced key macroeconomic variables such as consumption, investment and savings, as well as the idea of economic 'sectors'—households, businesses, governments and foreign economies—which affect an economy through their consumption, saving or investment of income, all of which are now important components of national accounting. It was the need to quantify these aggregates—to find a single numerical value for the sum of the billions and billions of transactions between buyers and sellers, savers and investors, that comprise the economy of a nation—that led Keynes to call in the late 1930s for the creation of national income accounts for Britain. With such a set of accounts economists would have a map to guide their policy; they would be able to 'survey and analyse an infinitely detailed and complex network of transactions within the economic unit constituted by a nation'.

Attempts to measure national income had been made as early as the 1660s by William Petty in England, but these early measures of national income were sporadic and isolated. And they were mere guesses: there was no systematic collection of information on national production by governments or any other institution. It was not until the depression of the 1930s that the idea of looking at a national economy in terms of accounting became widespread and the first attempts were made to calculate not just a nation's income but also its expenditure. The first official measure of the overall US economy—measures of national savings, consumption and investment—was devised by Simon Kuznets and his colleagues in the 1930s to provide policymakers with a comprehensive picture of what was going on. No comprehensive measures of national income and output had existed before then. It was the Depression that raised the need for national accounts such as the Gross Domestic Product (GDP)—or, as economist William D. Nordhaus said in 2010: 'If you want to know why GDP matters, you can just put yourself back in the 1930s period, where we had no idea what was happening to our economy.'

The first set of accounts—Kuznets' *National Income,*

1929–1932—was presented to Congress in 1934. It was a set of industry-by-industry estimates that amounted to 'national income'. Despite the concerns of Kuznets and his team that there were gaps in the data and other measurement uncertainties, these national income estimates were a major advance—and as a result of their construction Roosevelt was able to use national income statistics to describe the performance of the US economy from 1929 to 1937 in his April 1938 budget request to Congress.

The Second World War gave further urgency to the need for national income measurements. When the US economy was forced into wartime production in the 1940s, the measurements of output and income devised during the Depression were not enough: policymakers also needed information on US production and spending according to the types of products and purchases made so they could determine their wartime budgets. And so 'gross domestic product' estimates were calculated, to give the government a picture of the overall productive capacity of the economy and to show the impact on the economic state of the nation of a move from consumer spending on goods and services to federal government spending on tanks, materials and other requirements of war. This early measure of gross national expenditure gradually evolved into the Gross National Product (GNP), a term invented by Kuznets. GNP refers to the Gross Domestic Product (GDP) plus total capital gains from overseas investment less the income earned locally by foreign nationals (where GDP is the estimated value of the total worth of a country's annual production and services).

Back in England as war became imminent, Keynes was able to demonstrate that his new aggregate approach to a national economy could be applied not just to the problem of unemployment but also to the problem of managing a war economy, with its accompanying risks of inflation due to the sudden surge in government spending war necessitates. His method of combating inflation required the construction of national income statistics to manage aggregate demand. That is, assuming the extra government spending (or increased demand) in the wartime economy would cause inflation, Keynes wanted to control the economy's total demand (made up of demand from various sectors including consumers, business and government). To do so he needed a way to measure this total or aggregate demand, which can be approximated through national income statistics.

In February 1940, hoping to gain an official role in the wartime government, Keynes published his pamphlet *How to Pay for the War* as an appeal to the British Treasury to consider his radical ideas and, like the United States, gather statistics on the national economy so it would have a map to guide its financing of the war. Skidelsky calls *How to Pay for the War* arguably 'the quintessence of Keynes's achievement'. At its heart was Keynes's understanding that 'modern society would no longer stand "Nature's cures" of inflation and unemployment for the malfunctioning of the market system'. In other words, modern society required government intervention to moderate rampant market capitalism and minimise the ills of inflation and unemployment. It was for this landmark 1940 pamphlet that Keynes first developed a system of national accounts for the United Kingdom based on double-entry bookkeeping, a system which was published as the appendix 'A Budget of National Resources'. The budget was based on his *General Theory* concepts of aggregate demand and aggregate supply, measured in prices and subdivided into components—'to which he applied the golden rule of double-entry book-keeping, that the sums on both sides of the ledger must balance'.

Three months after *How to Pay for the War* was published, Germany invaded Belgium, Holland and France, Winston Churchill became Prime Minister— and Keynes was given an office in the British Treasury Chambers. His Treasury role was informal, but at last he had infiltrated the inner financial sanctum of the British wartime government. By January 1941, Keynes's call for a set of British national accounts had been answered and accomplished. Britain's inaugural set of national accounts was constructed by a team led by James Meade and Richard Stone at the Central Economic Information Service of the Offices of the War Cabinet and presented in the first draft of their paper 'National Income, Saving and Consumption', a survey of Britain's economic and financial situation. Their accounting framework reported net national income, net national output and net national expenditure; their tables reported macro-economic aggregates and showed the links between them.

In his 1984 Nobel Prize acceptance speech, Sir Richard Stone recalled his work on the wartime accounts in the early 1940s: 'Our estimates consisted of three tables relating to the national income and expenditure, personal income, expenditure and saving, and the net amount of funds required by, and available from, private sources for government purposes. They hardly amounted to a set of national accounts but they were a beginning.'

The government budget that followed in April 1941 was shaped largely by these statistics and the influence of Keynes. As Stone remembers, through Keynes's advocacy their rudimentary accounts were published as the second part of a White Paper called *An Analysis of the Sources of War Finance and an Estimate of the National Income and Expenditure in 1938 and 1940*, which accompanied the budget of 1941. This was an historic moment: it was the first practical application of Keynes's new analytic technique, which conceived the whole economy as a balance between total current resources (including real gross national product) on the supply side and total consumption, investment and expenditure for the war effort on the demand side. This was a radical shift because although earlier attempts had been made to measure national income, they had been mere guesses. Keynes devised a conceptual apparatus for understanding the working of an entire economy. Before this, governments did not systematically intervene to direct the economic affairs of nations (with notable exceptions such as the economic experiment being conducted contemporaneously in the Soviet Union).

Stone's experiments with processing the mass of statistics into structured national accounts prompted Keynes to say, not without irony, 'We are in a new era of joy through statistics'. As a thinker of great depth and complexity who saw economics above all as a moral practice, Keynes was suspicious of statistics and considered these quantitative measures of the national economy as exceptional, emergency measures demanded by the times. In the budget speech which presented these accounts for the first time, the British Chancellor expressed the same view, stressing that the publication of official estimates of national income and expenditure should not be regarded as setting a precedent. They were merely an exceptional measure made necessary by war. But as it turned out, they became an annual event and have become increasingly elaborate over the subsequent years.

And so the 'aggregate concepts' Keynes devised in the *General Theory* led directly to the development of Britain's national accounts in the 1940s and to the policies of 'demand management' for which he is now best known and which constitute the basis of 'Keynesian' economics. A new generation of economists, disciples of Keynes, subsequently converted his theory into a mathematical system which could be expressed as simultaneous equations (rather than the indeterminate system 'fraught with uncertainty and animal spirits' that Keynes himself had conceived and valued). This new framework and system of equations gave economists both a practical tool—fiscal policy (government spending and revenues)—with which to manipulate an economy, and, potentially, a central role in all future governments.

And so Venetian bookkeeping crossed yet another border to become an essential tool of national government. As one observer—Everett Hagen in *The Accounting Review*—described it in 1949, national accounting was 'the application of accounting principles to an entire economic organisation'. According to Hagen, 'national income measurement is best thought of as double-entry bookkeeping, involving the consolidation of the operating accounts of all productive enterprises in the economic system, including government'. Accounting historian Richard Mattessich expressed a similar view. He believed the term 'national accounting' acknowledges that macro- (or whole-economy) economics is in fact a kind of accounting, and argued that it is distinct from business and other micro-accounting systems 'only by a higher degree of aggregation and a somewhat different technique in collecting and processing data'.

The postwar global economy

~

Towards the end of the war, Keynes proposed the idea of an international clearing bank to ease the transition from a war economy to peacetime. He was especially concerned that member countries with balance of payments surpluses might hoard their wealth to the detriment of those countries who faced deficits following their enormous wartime expenditures, reigniting the threat of unemployment. The bank would work to offset this by maintaining balance of payments equilibriums (an equivalence between the wealth flowing into and out of a nation) between each member country and the rest of the world. As Skidelsky says, for Keynes the 'real "heart of the matter"—in global as well as in domestic policy—was to prevent unemployment by reducing the attractions of holding money'.

Keynes's idea was taken up in Washington, but remodelled in favour of the United States (just as Keynes's original concept had favoured the British Empire) and transformed into two international bodies: the Bank for Reconstruction and Development (which became the World Bank) and the International Monetary Fund (IMF). It was the creation of these and other international organisations after the Second World War that made the gathering of national income statistics an essential task for every nation involved and prompted an era of national income accounting. Accounting became an essential component of national and international government.

With this in mind, in 1944 Stone was sent to America to discuss his work on national income and expenditure estimates with his counterparts in the United States and Canada, in the hope that together they could adjust their various approaches to make their national tables comparable.

Attempts to achieve international harmony and comparability in national accounting methods became even more pressing with the end of the war, especially because they were then linked to the operation of the Marshall Plan (US monetary assistance with the rebuilding of the economies of Europe) and the funding of the postwar reconstruction of much of Europe and Asia generally. The Organisation for European Economic Co-operation (OEEC) was established in Paris with the initial aim of administering American aid under the Marshall Plan. It was decided that national accounts would be used as the framework for reviewing the progress of member countries. Under the aegis of the newly created United Nations, Stone was put in charge of an international group of experts to compile standardised forms of national accounting which could be recommended for international use. He was made responsible for achieving three things for the United Nations: producing a standard system of national accounts, preparing studies of the national accounts of individual countries, and training other statisticians.

The work of Stone and his colleagues first appeared as an appendix—'Measurement of National Income and the Construction of Social Accounts'—to a report published by the United Nations (UN) in Geneva in 1947. The UN then published it in 1952 as *A System of National Accounts and Supporting Tables* as part of its 'Standardised System of National Accounts'. As the first ever attempt to standardise national accounting practice across the world, the UN's System of National Accounts (SNA) automatically became best international practice.

In 1952, very few statisticians were familiar with the theory and practice of national accounting. This would soon change irrevocably. The work done by Stone, Kuznets and others became the foundation of international accounting, and their national income statistics used to measure economic growth would soon become *the* key indicator of national success and government performance.

The SNA has been refined and expanded periodically since its original construction. A new system was published in 1968 with contributions from experts from around the world chaired by Stone. The report explained the need for standardised and comparable national accounts as follows: 'by providing a consistent picture of the development of an economic system, a series of national accounts are useful, indeed indispensable, in describing and analyzing economic change and so contribute to many forms of economic decision making'.

The SNA was revised again in 1993 because of the increasing complexity of economic and financial systems, and the myriad changes brought by rapid technological advances, such as electronic transfer mechanisms, intellectual capital, financial services and other intangible activities. The new framework was widely supported by the UN, the European Economic Community, the IMF, the World Bank and the Organisation for Economic Co-operation and Development (OECD).

Since the 1950s, Stone's double-entry national accounting systems have become crucial economic tools for national governments, used to analyse economic cycles and as the basis of national budget planning and forecasts. They are also now indispensable in international economic management. These supposedly comparable national accounting statistics have since their inception guided the policies of international organisations such as the various UN agencies, the OECD and the World Bank.

Thus economic growth—as calculated by Gross National Product (GNP) and other national income statistics—became a key measure of the success of nations and central to the operation of the new postwar international financial institutions developed under the guidance of John Maynard Keynes. Today the statistics generated by national income accounts are a regular and essential feature of our economic and financial landscape. Their value for corporations is explained by Laura D'Andrea Tyson, Dean of the School of Business at the University of California at Berkeley:

The quality of business decisions depends
on information—more information means
less uncertainty and better decisions. The US
national income accounts provide business
leaders with critical information about the
trends shaping their market opportunities
and challenges. These accounts are a critical
component of the institutional infrastructure
on which the health of our market economy
depends.

And US Senator Paul Sarbanes describes the central place national accounting has in the government of the United States: 'The GDP accounts provide Congress and the rest of government with vital signs on our economy's health. We are making better economic policy today because the GDP accounts give us a better understanding of what policies work.' US Senator Pete V. Domenici concurs: 'The ability to measure our economy accurately is abso-lutely critical in the formulation of the federal budget. Indeed, it would be difficult for government to function today without the excellent information provided by the Commerce Department's GDP series.' Economists Paul A. Samuelson and William D. Nordhaus call the GDP and other national accounts 'truly among the great inventions of the twentieth century'.

This is how in the twentieth century, double-entry bookkeeping became a measure not only of the wealth of firms and corporations, but also of the wealth of nations.

But the accuracy and usefulness of national income measures have been questioned from the beginning, by Keynes and others, including Simon Kuznets himself. For example, Kuznets believed the national accounts should include the value of unpaid housework, despite the fact that including this vast contribution to the national economy would present statisticians with the difficult task of making monetary estimates of this valuable work. The US Commerce Department refused to calculate these estimates—and as a result Kuznets broke his association with the department in the late 1940s.

Kuznets was also concerned about the effects on people's lives of the modern economic growth that these statistics encourage as an end in itself. As he explained in 1971, many costs of economic development—such as those related to migration and the retraining required by technological advances—

> are not now included in economic
> measurement, and some . . . may never
> be susceptible to measurement. Internal
> migration, from the countryside to the cities
> (within a country, and often international)
> represented substantial costs in the pulling up
> of roots and the adjustment to the anonymity
> and higher costs of urban living. The learning
> of new skills and the declining value of
> previously acquired skills was clearly a costly
> process—to both the individuals and to society.

Concerns about the bias and partiality of national accounting figures and the shortcomings of economic growth as a true measure of prosperity have continued to provoke debate. But before we can consider possible new measures and the future of national accounting, we must examine the extraordinary rise of corporate accounting over the twentieth century. For despite recurrent corporate collapses and jaw-dropping accounting scandals, accounting's rise since the profession received its first charter in the 1850s has been unstoppable.

THE RISE AND SCANDALOUS
RISE OF A PROFESSION

It would be interesting to know how many of those
whose hearts leap up at the announcement of an
increase in earnings per share have any idea of the
estimates, judgments, and conventions that must go
into all such calculations.

HOWARD ROSS

All right, but apart from the extra jobs, higher
profits, record fees, higher standards, cool image,
greater visibility, more shareholder protection,
better behaviour, enhanced ethical codes, us being
taken seriously, and gripping drama, what has
Enron done for us?

ACCOUNTANT, CHARACTER IN A PLAY

DATED APRIL 2001, ENRON'S ANNUAL REPORT FOR
the year 2000 exuded success. Profits were boom-
ing. Sales had soared from US$2.3 billion to over
US$100 billion in just four years. Income before interest
and taxes had risen by 72 per cent. Its top 140 executives

were paid an average of US$5.3 million each. But Enron was not just about profit. It also trumpeted its 'risk management skills that enable us to offer reliable prices as well as reliable delivery'. The market lapped it up. Share prices were high and *Fortune* magazine rated Enron 'America's Most Innovative Company' for the sixth consecutive year, and 'No. 1 in Quality of Management'.

Seven months later, Enron filed for bankruptcy. The golden goose of corporate capitalism collapsed amid charges of 'greed, bribery, corruption, deceit, parasitism, speculation, insider trading, scams, nepotism, tax avoidance, environmental destruction, human rights abuses, exploitation, theft of workers' entitlements, job losses, use of state machinery against workers and Indigenous peoples, cosy relationships with government, and monopoly manipulation of prices and markets'. How apt then that when chairman Kenneth Lay had renamed the provincial gas company 'Enron' a decade earlier, he had originally wanted to call it Enteron—until the *Wall Street Journal* pointed out that 'enteron' was a Greek-derived word for intestines.

Enron's spectacular profits were dependent on massive debts not recorded on the company's books. Instead, the debt was recorded in (off-the-books) subsidiaries or 'special purpose entities' (SPEs) and partnerships. Enron's debt was not US$13 billion as it appeared in its accounts. It was actually US$38 billion. It had understated its debt by a phenomenal US$25 billion.

Although hidden from the market, Enron's complex

financial manoeuvrings had not gone unnoticed. Before the scandal, senior Enron employee Sherron Watkins had written an anonymous letter to Kenneth Lay about her concerns: Watkins wondered whether the complex and mostly undisclosed deals had helped to inflate Enron's share price and would eventually be revealed as an 'elaborate accounting hoax'. She feared the company would 'implode in a wave of accounting scandals'. She was right. And she was ignored.

Enron's chief operating officer Jeffrey K. Skilling announced his resignation, apparently out of the blue, on 14 August 2001. On 16 October the company reported a US\$618 million third-quarter loss and a US\$1.2 billion reduction in shareholder equity. In October 2001, once the full magnitude of its accounting hoax had dawned on the market, Enron's share price began to plummet, but senior management forced Enron employees to hold their Enron shares until they hit 76 cents (from their high of over US\$90). Employees discovered their pension fund had been 'locked down' (62 per cent of the retirement assets of Enron's employees in the US were invested in Enron stock). Lay, on the other hand, was able to sell off more than US\$200 million worth of share options. As one employee recalled: 'Ken Lay knew the ship was sinking, yet he kept telling us to buy Enron stock. They were siphoning off our retirement funds to keep the ship afloat. When our Enron stock hit 76 cents a share, they emailed us and said we were now free to sell them.' On 2 December 2001, Enron filed for bankruptcy.

By the end of the year its shares were worth just 30 cents. It turned out the global energy company had also overstated its profits by over US$1 billion.

Enron had not always been a global giant. It had started out as a small gas company in Omaha, Nebraska—until Kenneth Lay renamed it and moved its headquarters to the more salubrious Houston, Texas. In 1992 the US energy industry was deregulated and government price controls were removed—and, advised by McKinsey consultant Jeffrey K. Skilling (who would join Enron in 1997), Lay set out to revolutionise the energy industry. Enron's share price boomed (from US$20 in 1997 to over US$90 in 2000), and by the end of 2000 it was the fourth largest company in the United States.

The collapse of this behemoth was followed by a wave of corporate accounting scandals so enormous that *Forbes* magazine compiled 'The Corporate Scandal Sheet' in 2002 to keep track of them all. But these were nothing compared with what was to come: the global financial crisis unleashed in 2008. On 26 February 2009, the largest company in the world by asset size, the Royal Bank of Scotland (RBS), gave a preliminary announcement of its annual results. It had lost £24 billion, the greatest loss in British corporate history. By June 2009, British taxpayers had spent £45.5 billion to bail out the RBS and another £50 billion for a toxic assets protection scheme—and, on top of that, a ludicrous £16 million payout to its disgraced former chief executive officer Sir Fred Goodwin. But in the bank's financial report published in February 2008—just seven weeks before it was forced to seek £12 billion in new capital—there is no evidence of its unsustainable financial position. There is something deeply wrong with a system in which company accounts, required by law to give a true picture of a corporation's financial position for investors, are inscrutable. As John Lanchester says: 'The experience of reading a publicly held company's accounts is not supposed to resemble a first encounter with the late Mallarmé', the notoriously difficult French symbolist poet.

And yet compared to some companies, the RBS accounts are 'models of clarity and translucency'. With the creation of the derivatives market and other complex financing tools in the 1980s, company accounts have become ever more opaque. As American industrialist and investor Warren Buffett wrote in 2004: 'No matter how financially sophisticated you are, you can't possibly learn from reading the disclosure documents of a derivatives-intensive company what risks lurk in its positions. Indeed, the more you know about derivatives, the less you will feel you can learn from the disclosures normally proffered you.'

The collapse of massive enterprises like Enron and the Royal Bank of Scotland raises serious questions about the culture that allows such organisations to flourish and their executives to profit at the expense of thousands of shareholders and employees—and taxpayers. In particular, especially given that the Enron case was followed by the demise of its accountant and auditor

Arthur Andersen, it raises questions about the accounting and auditing of corporations in general, particularly of large multinational companies whose complex and exotic accounting practices obscure their true financial state and make possible these sudden and spectacular failures.

But despite the serious questions such scandals raise about the value of contemporary corporate accounting, in practice these frauds act like fertiliser on the accounting profession, causing accountants to spring up in ever greater numbers and their profession to flourish.

Before I started researching it, I had intended to name this chapter 'The rise and fall of a profession'. It was to chart the glorious rise of accounting in the second half of the twentieth century to the lofty heights of the professional Olympus and then trace its collapse in the wake of scandals like Enron and WorldCom, and in Australia, HIH, One.Tel and ABC Learning. However, not only has no such fall ensued but it turns out that these accounting scandals are a regular feature in the landscape of accounting. They are as old as the profession itself, dating back to the earliest days of the formalised use of collective capital: the corporation. Corporations and accounting scandals go together like Gordon Gekko and greed. The nineteenth and early twentieth centuries are rife with corporate collapses of the magnitude of Enron's and comparable in their elements. And they all stem from significant accounting misstatements orchestrated by influential senior managers. Equally, the responses of lawmakers and watchdogs have been the same over the past one hundred years: tinker around the edges of the law, found new watchdogs, proclaim a new era of greater scrutiny and let accountants and auditors out to play with the managers of vast sums of other people's money. Never are the fundamentals of this arrangement questioned—the corporate structure itself or the role of accountants as its referees.

Given that modern corporations are now so complex that even gurus like Warren Buffett warn that some of their practices, such as derivatives, are inscrutable, should we not be asking whether it is actually possible to construct a set of financial statements that summarise in a few numbers the vast range and complexity of a corporation's annual activity? And whether this can be done just weeks after the financial year ends, and to such high standards that they are taken seriously by the market and those who need to assess the progress of the corporation? The miracles abound.

From the Industrial Revolution to the twenty-first century, company financial accounts have painted misleading pictures by manipulating expense and revenue figures and using complex business group structures to obscure the true financial condition of an organisation. As we have seen, it was from government intervention in this errant corporate activity that the modern accounting profession—and its regulation—has evolved. The requirement that company accounts be audited was a chief component of this regulation. It seems, however, that in the nineteenth century a culture of 'auditing excuses' was created, which permitted accountants to deny a primary responsibility for detecting accounting irregularities perpetrated by management, and this culture continues today. Auditors were required by law to focus exclusively on accounting records and the balance sheet, and not to question the honesty of senior managers or tell them how to manage. In 1890s Britain, two cases (*London and General Bank* and *Kingston Cotton Mill*) popularised the audit mantra of 'reasonable care and skill in the circumstances' as the basic model to excuse corporate auditors from detecting accounting misstatements. Today these precedents are enshrined in legislation: management, not the auditors, 'is responsible for accounting systems and therefore for preventing and detecting fraudulent activity through internal control systems'.

In the 1920s the US construction business Kreuger & Toll became one of the largest conglomerates and multinationals imaginable, like Enron seventy years later. After its founder Ivar Kreuger died in 1932, millions of investors discovered the company's financial statements had been falsified over many years. But because of the company's extraordinary organisational complexity, the investigating accountants Price Waterhouse could not determine the exact extent of the fraud and so the investors lost their money. The Wall Street Crash of 1929 revealed the accounts of another titanic company, Insull Utility Investments, to be 'grossly misleading'. Its CEO Samuel Insull was tried for fraud in 1932 and acquitted on all counts. A considerable part of Insull's defence rested on the persuasiveness of the commonsense rationale behind his accounting practices (he had treated stock dividends as income, which was prohibited at the time, but the prosecution was unable to make a clear case against it)—and, by implication, 'the financial nonsense peddled in the conventional accounting wisdom'. The prosecution was left without a case, unable to deny that the accounting rules of the day were controversial and unable to claim that there was any consensus within the accounting profession on the particular rule in question. The Insull case highlighted the contentious and arbitrary nature of corporate accounting, especially regarding valuation and depreciation, issues which are essentially unresolvable and continue to be hotly debated today. Significantly, some of Insull's accounting practices, which then lay outside conventional accounting practice, are now accepted wisdom.

These and other corporate scandals led in 1929 to a new Companies Act in Britain and to Roosevelt's New Deal in the United States, which created the Securities and Exchange Commission (SEC) in 1934 to regulate the securities industry and enforce federal laws. The reporting of a profit and loss account—or income statement—became legally required in the UK. In the United States the Securities Acts of 1933 and 1934 mandated audited financial statements for all publicly traded companies. Again, this legislation had the effect of further enhancing the role of accountants, as accounting historians Thomas A. Lee, Frank L. Clarke and Graeme W. Dean argue: 'The impact of the Securities and Exchange Commission on the US accounting profession has been incalculable. For one, the Securities Acts formalised the audit process, limited its practice to CPAs, and glamorised that side of the profession.' By the end of the 1930s the income statement had become the focal point of US accounting practice and reflected the growing importance of equity markets and shareholders as providers of finance.

THE BURGEONING COMPLEXITY AND
AVAILABILITY OF ACCOUNTING INFORMATION

The development of computers during the Second World War allowed unprecedented leaps in the amount of financial data that could be generated to feed the voracious appetite of financial markets for such information. Until the end of the nineteenth century, accounting had been a slow, painstaking, labour-intensive manual process: transactions were entered by hand into large bound journals which were then posted by hand to large bound ledgers. The first major innovations in information processing came in the 1870s. With the introduction of calculating machines, including the recording adding machine introduced by William S. Burroughs (the Beat poet William

Burroughs' grandfather), accounting became somewhat faster and more standardised. The preparation of trial balances became more common, data analysis became easier—and so more and more financial data was created and used.

After the Second World War, accountants were a driving force behind the adoption of computers by businesses—and their own need to process information ever more quickly and efficiently spurred further development of the computer. In 1954 Arthur Andersen & Co. advised General Electric to buy its first computer—the UNIVAC—to process its business information and accounts. By 1970, computers had become essential for most larger corporations and reduced many accounting tasks from weeks to mere hours. And with the development of the internet, financial information became instantly accessible around the globe 24 hours a day. With computerisation, the internet and the deregulated international economy, the demand for financial information has exploded—and the accounting profession has expanded accordingly.

But computerisation is an auditor's nightmare: it replaces most physical records with electronic data which is potentially easier to lose track of, and has meant accounting firms have had to rethink the audit process. Essentially they have done so by attempting to establish more comprehensive accounting systems that are easier to check and safeguard, and by implementing rigorous internal company controls.

The increased significance—glamour, even—of accounting information and financial reporting is reflected in the massive investment that companies now make in the presentation of their own financial reports. By the 1970s public companies were beginning to use their annual reports as much as a tool for public relations—to communicate new concepts like 'corporate identity', for example—as for delivering financial accounts and other information. They exploited the latest technologies—first in paper production, photolithography and typography, later in electronic communications and the internet—and invested thousands of dollars to produce professionally designed, visually appealing reports. The design innovations of annual reports often express the changing fortunes of the market: for example, the British clothing company Burton PLC produced lavish fashion-related annual reports during the high-rolling, bullish 1980s and then matched the mood of the more straitened, bearish early 1990s with reports in sombre grey minimalism.

Accounting's forward-looking postwar exuberance—with its extended functions of management consultancy, forecasting and business planning, rather than its former cautious, past-oriented image associated with auditing—was also seen in the extensions made in the 1960s to the London headquarters of the Institute of Chartered Accountants in England and Wales (ICAEW). As we've seen, these were the same headquarters that had been built during the profession's infancy in the 1880s, but the

'Brutalist' additions—geometric slabs of concrete and glass—designed by avant-garde architect William Whitfield updated the nineteenth-century ICAEW building to articulate accountancy's new, more future-oriented role. According to one commentator, Whitfield transformed the original building 'into a Janus-like structure which embraced the future while revering and claiming links with accountancy's long history'.

POSTWAR REGULATION

As the modern corporation grew increasingly complex in the postwar era, it became apparent that legislative responses to accounting scandals had been inadequate. And so new standard-setting organisations were established in the United Kingdom and the United States: the Accounting Standards Steering Committee (later the Accounting Standards Committee (ASC)) was set up in the UK in 1970 and three years later the Financial Accounting Standards Board (FASB) was established in the US. These bodies increasingly codified accounting practices, especially the meaning of 'true and fair view' (one of accounting's most fundamental principles, thought to be achieved when a company's accounts give a correct and complete picture of its financial position) and 'generally accepted accounting principles' (accounting standards within any particular jurisdiction). The globalisation of capital markets and the growing need for internationally acceptable accounting standards led to the creation of an international accounting body in 1973: the International Accounting Standards Committee, which was replaced in 2001 by the International Accounting Standards Board (IASB).

But more regulation and further standardisation of the accounting profession did nothing to avert or even to diminish accounting-related corporate scandals. In 1991, the Bank of Credit and Commerce International (BCCI) was forced to close when its auditors Price Waterhouse discovered a billion-dollar fraud in its accounts. But what exactly had gone on in the books of BCCI may never be known, because its multinational corporate structure was so intricate and labyrinthine that no individual jurisdiction was fully aware of what the company was doing. The 1990s also saw the spectacular crashes of the Maxwell Communications Corporation and Polly Peck International empire in the UK.

The global financial community had hardly recovered from the shock of Enron's seismic collapse in 2001 when another corporate scandal was revealed. When the telecommunications giant WorldCom declared bankruptcy in 2002 with an apparent US$11 billion in accounting irregularities (as with Enron, its auditor was Arthur Andersen), it was one of the largest corporations in the United States.

The fortunes of corporate Australia have been similarly scandal filled. In 1963, one of Australia's largest retailers, Reid Murray Holdings, went into receivership.

But CEO Oswald O'Grady was charged merely with being an 'inept manager' and 'an artless victim of his own incompetence'. Three decades later the head of the failed Bond Corporation, Alan Bond, was not let off so easily. Bond was found guilty of Australia's largest corporate fraud, the so-called Bond Corp/Bell Resources 'cash cow transactions' (a secret loan scheme to strip Bell Resources of more than AU$1.2 billion), and sentenced to seven years in prison.

In the twenty-first century, the collapse in 2001 of Ray Williams' HIH, Australia's biggest insurance company, with an estimated deficiency of over AU$5 billion became one of Australia's most notorious corporate scandals. In 2003 the HIH Royal Commission Report concluded that: 'despite (myriad governance) mechanisms the corporate officers, auditors and regulators of HIH failed to see, remedy or report . . . [the] obvious. This was a situation not assisted by the dominance of HIH CEO and founder Ray Williams. Williams might be considered the epitome of the dominant senior manager genre.' It appears that Williams controlled the HIH board—and possibly even the company's auditor, Arthur Andersen, although no charges were laid against Arthur Andersen. The high-profile collapse of the telecommunications company One.Tel reportedly cost investors around AU$900 million, but there was little public suggestion that its accounting did not comply with Australian accounting standards.

More recently, the sudden demise of Eddy Groves'

childcare operator ABC Learning revealed serious accounting anomalies. The company's last detailed financial statements—the accounts for the half-year ending 31 December 2007—were delivered in February 2008. ABC Learning had a new auditor, Ernst & Young, whose interpretation of these accounts was profoundly different from the company's previous auditor, Pitcher Partners, who had endorsed management's upbeat interpretation of the corporation's health. Contrary to management and Pitcher Partners' view, Ernst & Young found the company's supposedly skyrocketing profits were mired in losses that would easily wipe out any profits the company ever made.

The demise of ABC Learning is similar to the cases of HIH and One.Tel. All three companies attempted to expand their market share as rapidly as possible, a strategy which entailed significant risks which were not clearly reflected in their financial statements, as head of accounting at the University of Western Sydney Philip Ross explains. The risk inherent in the business practices of ABC Learning had been pointed out to the Australian Securities and Investments Commission (ASIC) in 2006 by a complainant in the following statement: 'It's suggested that the methods of financial reporting being employed here are designed to artificially create apparent shareholder value, when, in fact, that shareholder value associated with the child-care licences (92 percent of net assets) is based entirely on future net cash flows of the company, which may or may not be realised.'

Needless to say, accounting for future possible cash flows in the company's present assets is seriously misleading to potential investors. But instead of acknowledging this, ASIC, the national watchdog, replied in 2006: 'after carefully considering the results of these inquiries, ASIC will not be taking any further action in relation to the issues you have raised'.

When the board of ABC Learning realised how vastly different Ernst & Young's reading of their financial situation was from Pitcher Partners', they called in a neutral third party, KPMG, to examine the accounts. The result? KPMG could fault neither Pitcher Partners' nor Ernst & Young's radically different interpretations. As it turned out, Ernst & Young's interpretation was the correct one. Its reading of the accounts alone diagnosed 'what was ultimately a fatal condition'. How could two professional account readings be so substantially at odds and yet both be declared apparently faultless? According to experts, the case raises two issues: one is the 'audit expectations gap' and the other is the ability of directors to oversee their companies' accounting practices. The 'audit expectations gap' refers to the discrepancy between the common but wrong public belief that auditors guarantee the rectitude of accounts, that they thoroughly check every detail of corporate accounts and certify them, and the reality, that in fact auditors are required merely to check the accounts enough to assure themselves they are okay. Auditors express an opinion only; they guarantee nothing. The other problem is with company directors being charged with corporate governance—which means they must oversee the accounting of their own firms. Ross says that cases like that of ABC Learning raise questions about how able directors are to carry out their corporate governance roles, given the complexity of contemporary business structures and operations, and the range of accounting approaches it is possible to adopt. He argues that 'what it comes down to is accounting policy choice and this is where you can get differences in interpretation'. Perhaps after all there is not such a vast chasm separating the astrological mathematics of Pacioli's day from the mathematics of contemporary accounting practice.

The director of Melbourne University's Centre for Corporate Law, Ian Ramsay, says the ABC Learning case reflects the recent move from accounting standards towards principles-based accounting, which allows auditors and accountants more latitude in how they address different accounting situations: 'In a fast-moving market it's impossible to draft accounting standards to cover every contingency.' This is understandable. But the trade-off for this flexibility in the rapidly changing commercial and financial environment is that 'strong enforcement' is needed to keep auditors honest—and it seems this is not often forthcoming.

Pitcher Partners has the last (eyebrow-raising) word on the accounts of the failed company: 'The Pitcher Partners Brisbane firm stands by its audit of ABC

Learning and notes that the application of accounting standards is subject to interpretation and professional judgement.'

REGULATION IN THE NEW MILLENNIUM
~

Although Enron's accounting practice was arguably no more devious than that of many of its contemporaries, it was 'the straw that broke the corporate camel's back'—Enron was possibly too big and allegedly too well connected with Congress and the Bush administration to ignore. Its collapse, followed so soon by WorldCom's and several other accounting scandals, led to the US Sarbanes-Oxley Act of 2002 which introduced major changes to the regulation of financial practice and corporate governance, as well as a public company accounting oversight board to oversee the auditors of public companies.

Section 1102 of the Act outlines fines and prison terms for those who tamper with the transactional records of a firm. Enron's chief operating officer Jeffrey K. Skilling was sentenced to 24 years under its terms. The company's auditor Arthur Andersen admitted to shredding Enron working papers and was liquidated in 2003. When senior Enron employee Sherron Watkins testified to the House Energy and Commerce Committee, she suggested that Kenneth Lay had not understood Enron's trading and accounting practices, and that Skilling and chief financial officer Andrew Fastow had an intimidating management style. Fastow was found guilty of fraud and entered a plea bargain. Lay was found guilty of all six charges against him but died before sentencing. The CEO of WorldCom, Bernie Ebbers, was given a 25-year sentence.

While these and other charges were prestigious 'heads on poles' for regulators, these punishments did not address the need for the reform of corporate financial reporting itself. Analysis of the Enron case has suggested its accounting was 'grossly deviant due to managerial manipulation'—but in fact much of its accounting, including its contentious 'mark-to-model' techniques (the practice of pricing a position or portfolio according to abstract financial models rather than the market) and debt-loaded SPEs, had been approved by the SEC and the FASB.

The Australian federal government's response to corporate accounting malpractice following the failure of HIH and One.Tel in 2001 was similar to that of the US government: it commissioned an inquiry and targeted corporate managers. But the convictions and sentences given to HIH's Ray Williams and Rodney Adler (on charges not directly linked to HIH's collapse) were relatively minor compared to those given in the US. ASIC's action to recover AU$92 million from One.Tel's Jodee Rich and Mark Silberman for allegedly overseeing trading when the company was insolvent was unsuccessful, although it did reveal how 'aggressive accounting' can conceal insolvency.

Australia committed to the international financial reporting standards (IFRS) in a 2005 Australian version—although according to a KPMG survey of Australian insurance companies, two-thirds of the respondents believed this commitment would increase the risk of inaccuracy in financial reporting. The US Securities and Exchange Commission has accepted IFRS standards since March 2008—but they do not yet apply to US corporations.

A CERTAIN CIRCULARITY

~

While the post-2000 push for tighter corporate governance might suggest a new era in regulation, arguably these episodes are little more than replays of responses to the many instances of scandalous corporate behaviour that have occurred over the past one hundred and seventy or so years. Current concern about the usefulness of financial statements for revealing corporate wealth and progress is very similar to that expressed a century ago. Former US president George W. Bush's post-Enron resolve to clean up corporate America was remarkably similar to Roosevelt's 'truth in securities' vow following the Great Crash of 1929. In Roosevelt's day, the corporate villain was Samuel Insull. In Bush's, the bad guys were Kenneth Lay, Jeffrey Skilling and Arthur Andersen. Ironically, while Enron's collapse brought about the demise of Arthur Andersen, Roosevelt had set up Andersen as auditing's rising star when he appointed the then small firm to investigate the failure of the Insull empire.

The 2008 global financial crisis revealed the gaping holes in the Sarbanes-Oxley Act a mere six years after Bush signed it into law. President Barack Obama's 2010 vow to reform Wall Street with the Dodd-Frank Wall Street Reform and Consumer Protection Act has been similarly lauded, celebrated in Congress and the media as the most far-reaching regulatory overhaul since the Great Depression. But as former chairman of the US Federal Reserve Paul Volcker observed before Obama signed the legislation on 21 July 2010: 'There is a certain circularity in all this business. You have a crisis, followed by some kind of reform, for better or worse, and things go well for a while, and then you have another crisis.'

It seems something is fundamentally wrong here. A century and a half of corporate accounting scandals say that financial reporting does not present a reliable picture of corporate wealth and progress, and that auditing does not protect shareholders from manipulative, self-interested managers charged with the care of their assets. Financial statements have failed dismally to reveal the true state of companies whose collapse is a hair's breadth away, such as Enron, WorldCom, HIH and One.Tel. They are neither 'transparent' nor 'truthful'. Despite the fact that accounting 'inaccuracies' go hand in hand with sudden corporate collapses and failures, accounting itself is never questioned. Accounting is never held to account. Little has changed since 1933, despite rhetoric, legislation and litigation. The answer to exactly how we should account for corporations appears to be as uncertain now as it was eighty years ago.

And what is true of accountants is also true of auditors. Auditors repeatedly fail to detect accounting irregularities and we see the same cycle of financial scandal followed by regulatory response in auditing. Ernst & Young, the auditors of the failed global financial services conglomerate Lehman Brothers, did not question inadequate disclosures in the bank's results. Arthur Andersen was complicit in the sudden collapse of Enron; the auditor both advised the company on how to set up its SPEs and audited the company's books. Such conflicts of interest are common, says Prem Sikka, professor of accounting at the University of Essex. Sikka calls auditors a 'weak link in this chain':

> you have one floor of big accountancy firms
> doing an audit and another floor giving advice
> on how to bypass rules and regulations and
> how to flatter their financial statements. And
> they make money whichever way things go.
> So they could check these things, but I think
> since they are profit-making entities there
> is very little impulse to check these things.
> Like Russian Roulette: 99 percent of the time
> you get away with it, and that's exactly what
> accountancy firms have been doing.

THE STATE OF THE INDUSTRY

~

The demise of Arthur Andersen in 2002 left four big international accounting firms: KPMG, PricewaterhouseCoopers, Deloitte Touche Tohmatsu and Ernst & Young. Together the 'Big Four' employ hundreds of thousands of people, have more offices around the world than Coca-Cola and an annual turnover of around US$90 billion—more than the GDP of many nations—which makes them collectively the world's fifty-fourth largest economy. But these global giants are not themselves required to provide audited financial statements and they publish only very limited accounts of their own. They have become rich from spreading the idea of league tables, which they conceive and run—for schools (such as MySchool), hospitals, universities—and yet there is no league table to assess their own performance.

Prem Sikka thinks the industry needs reforming. At the very least, he believes auditing should be taken over by a specially designated regulator, because accountancy firms have generally failed to deliver what the public expects of them. He also believes accounting firms should be opened to scrutiny. But in fact, the trend is in the opposite direction: accountancy firms are being granted more and more liability concessions, which makes it increasingly difficult for any aggrieved or injured stakeholder to sue them. Speaking in 2010, Sikka said he believes 'we will see more and more scandals around accounting and around the failures of auditors'.

Accounting's use of numbers gives it an air of scientific rectitude and certitude, and yet fundamental uncertainties lurk at its heart. Indeed, accounting is as subjective and partial as the art of storytelling, the other meaning contained in the word 'account'. For example, the tale of 'how Harold of Salisbury borrowed money to buy a new cow' becomes 'a debt for £2 10s', where this incident is extracted from its place and time in an ongoing saga of Harold's life to become timeless numbers grouped together in a table under abstract headings such as 'capital', 'wages' and 'income'. But just because the randomness and uncertainty inherent in the flux of life are transformed into the apparent solidity and certainty of numbers and charts does not mean that these numbers are any less selective or any less skewed to the narrator's point of view than was the original story.

Even accounting's most fundamental concepts and practices, such as income measurement and asset valuation, are based on uncertainties. Accountants still cannot agree on how to define income, the measurement of which remains one of the intractable problems in financial accounting theory and practice. The valuation of assets only becomes more complex and more fiercely debated as modern global corporate structures and financial instruments become increasingly labyrinthine, and income measurement, the key to determining profits and therefore dividends, is inextricably linked to this contentious, chimerical practice of asset valuation. Nor is the crucial measurement of costs an objective process: costs are also highly contestable figures and may result as much from the collusion or rivalries of firms as from any other actuality. Accrual (or corporate) accounting—the need to allocate revenues and expenses between accounting periods and to value assets and liabilities at the end of an accounting period—raises problems which have never been solved and are probably incapable of solution. Numbers can be negotiated to make management look good. In effect, 'accounts are used to justify decisions and to excuse mistakes'.

THE WIZARDS OF WALL STREET

And yet the figures produced by Pacioli's double-entry bookkeeping to create the four financial statements that are the raison d'être of modern accounting—the balance sheet, the income statement, the cash-flow statement and the statement of retained earnings—today run the international economy and drive its share markets. The importance of numbers such as EPS (earnings per share) reflects the increasing domination of capital markets and the globalisation of finance, and shifts focus from the balance sheet (and the ability to pay) to the income statement (and earnings capacity).

Today these numbers are manipulated by the powerful wizards of Wall Street, the mathematical geniuses who run the quantitative equity (or 'quant') funds, which rely on complex and sophisticated mathematical algorithms to find the glitches and anomalies, the hidden patterns in the markets, the infinitesimal stock movements and trends which yield their fortunes. Nassim Nicholas Taleb, the author of the bestselling book on improbability, *The Black Swan*, himself a former quant nerd, says of the quant nerds: 'Most are idiot savants brought to industrial proportions.' The elite funds run by these 'idiot savants' are called 'black-box' funds: 'opaque to outsiders, the boxes contain investment magic understood by only the wizards who conjured it up'.

As the *Washington Post*'s Frank Ahrens says, the allure of a unifying, perfect mathematical formula with which to generate a fortune from financial markets is powerful. It is as irresistible to the quant nerds as the formula for turning dross into gold was to the alchemists. The way Ahrens tells it, the magic of mathematics is as compelling in our day as it was in Pacioli's: 'Math's universal principles underlie and suffuse everyday life and the workings of the cosmos, offering a glimpse of the eternal. In the frequently irrational financial markets, mathematic models offer the hope of cool reason and certitude, a sort of godlike wisdom.' Employing the rhetoric of religion, Ahrens describes the high priest of the quants, James Simons, who works 'in a form of high math decipherable to a handful of humans on the planet. As such, practitioners of the rare mathematic arts can become the powerful priests of investing, thanks to their strange and obscure language, much the way the medieval church trafficked in Latin'.

The antics of the share market and its mathematical wizards manipulate not only the wealth of individuals and corporations, they also dramatically shape the political life of nations. Naomi Klein gives a stark example of the impact of markets on politics. Following the election of Nelson Mandela as President of South Africa, 'Every time a top party official said something that hinted that the ominous Freedom Charter might still become policy, the market responded with a shock, sending the rand into free fall. The rules were simple and crude, the electronic equivalent of monosyllabic grunts: justice—expensive, sell; status quo—good, buy.' The market proved to be the greatest constraint on Mandela's new government. As Klein says, 'this, in a way, is the genius of unfettered capitalism: it's self-enforcing'. Once a country is part of the global market, any failure to adhere to Chicago School orthodoxy (the neoclassical economic theories made popular by Milton Friedman which favour free markets and therefore limited government intervention) is immediately 'punished by traders in New York and London who bet against the offending country's currency, causing a deeper crisis and the need for more loans, with more conditions attached'.

THE CORPORATION

And what of the corporate form itself? Is it, like double-entry accounting, in need of radical reform?

Economist Raj Patel points out that while every civilisation has had traders and markets, only modern market
society has spawned the corporation, 'a novel human creation moved by the search for profit', which now dominates
the planet. Patel tells the story of a group of filmmakers
(Mark Achbar, Jennifer Abbott and Joel Bakan) who
decided to treat the corporation like the person it legally
is and test its psychological profile. Using the *American
Psychiatric Association's Diagnostic and Statistical Manual
of Mental Disorders* (DSM-IV), they found that the corporation shares many of the characteristics that define
psychopaths. That is, corporations break the law if they
can, they hide their behaviour, sacrifice long-term welfare for short-term profit, are aggressively litigious, ignore
health and safety codes, and cheat their suppliers and
workers without remorse. For example, in the 1960s the
agricultural company Monsanto poisoned the waterways
of Anniston, Alabama, ('fish died within ten seconds,
spurting blood and shedding skin') without the town
knowing, because it did not want to lose a single dollar in
business. When the case was tried in 2001, in its defence a
representative of the company said 'it was unfair to judge
the company's environmental performance in the 1970s
by modern standards'.

Such morally repugnant behaviour and disregard for
human life are not confined to the dark recesses of the
twentieth century. In the twenty-first century, in tapes
that were released in 2004, Enron is revealed as having
behaved in a similarly antisocial fashion. In order to

keep electricity prices—and hence their own profits—high, in 2000 Enron traders asked the El Paso Electric Company to shut down production. This led not only to high prices but to blackouts across California, which experienced 38 blackouts in the six months following the deregulation of the Californian electricity industry. This occurred not because there wasn't enough electricity to go around, but because Enron wanted to artificially inflate the price of electricity. In another of the tapes released in 2004, Enron employees are seen watching the Californian forest fires on television. As they watch they can be heard celebrating the destruction of electricity pylons and shouting, 'Burn, baby, burn!' All in the name of corporate profit.

But even when they go about their lawful business, corporations cause harm simply because of the way they—and profit-driven markets—value the world. In order for profits to be as high as possible, corporations keep costs as low as possible. The real costs of their business are higher than their stated costs—but they remain hidden. For example, Patel has estimated the real cost of a Big Mac to be US$200. The reason Big Macs sell for almost one-hundredth of this figure is that their drive-through price does not account for their real costs. These include their carbon footprint, their impact on the environment in terms of water use and soil degradation, and the enormous health costs of diet-related illnesses such as diabetes and heart disease. Traditional accounting models do not take these costs into account, but they still have to be paid. It is just that the McDonald's Corporation does not pay them. So, who does pay? We do. Society as a whole pays, in the form of environmental disasters, climate-change-related migration and higher health costs.

While the US$200 hamburger is an estimate, 'what is abundantly clear is that the market fails to account for all actual costs in the price we pay at the checkout counter'. As Patel sees it, the fact that corporations are not paying the environmental and social costs they rack up amounts to corporate subsidy on a massive scale: 'You'd be forgiven for thinking that this ongoing bailout from nature and society to private enterprise is what puts the "free" in free markets—despite its protests, corporate capitalism has yet to prove that it can operate without these kinds of subsidies.'

According to a recent study, the bill for the earth's degraded ecosystems could amount to US$47 trillion. While the fruits of this debt are mostly enjoyed by those of us who can afford to buy the goods produced by corporations—computers, t-shirts, toilet paper—the cost of the debt is unevenly spread across the world, mostly paid by the nations who can least afford it (such as in the desertification of Bolivia, the mudslides of Pakistan, the deforestation of the Amazon): 'The ecological debt of rich countries to poor ones [estimated at US$4.32 trillion] dwarfs the entire third-world debt owed by poor nations to rich ones, which is only US$1.8 trillion.'

Which brings us to the most pressing issue of the

day: the health of our planet. In the words of the *Economist*: 'There has been much hullabaloo about corporate accounting scams in America, yet perhaps the biggest accounting oversight of all time remains hidden in governments' own national figures. GDP per head is the most commonly used measure of a country's success, yet it is badly flawed as a guide to a nation's economic well being.' Yes, GDP is deeply flawed as a guide to a nation's wellbeing. And it also completely fails to account for the cost to the planet of economic growth.

GROSS DOMESTIC PRODUCT AND HOW ACCOUNTING COULD MAKE OR BREAK THE PLANET

... a country could exhaust its mineral resources,
cut down its forests, erode its soil, pollute its
aquifers, and hunt its wildlife to extinction, but
measured income would not be affected as these
assets disappeared ...

ROBERT REPETTO, WORLD RESOURCES INSTITUTE, 2000

These accounting systems evolved at a time when
the natural world seemed endless and our focus
was on managing the industrial revolution, not our
natural environment.

WENTWORTH GROUP OF CONCERNED SCIENTISTS, 2008

There is nothing immutable about the construction
of the national accounts, about what does and what
does not constitute economic activity.

PAUL ORMEROD, *THE DEATH OF ECONOMICS*, 1994

AS WE HAVE SEEN, NATIONAL ACCOUNTS WERE introduced in the United States and Britain in the 1930s and 40s as a measure for guiding governments through the Depression and financing the Second World War. They have since been developed and adopted throughout the world and now play a crucial role in international economic and political life. As economists Paul A. Samuelson and William D. Nordhaus explain, the GDP and related national accounting data have been used as 'beacons that help policymakers steer the economy toward the key economic objectives'. These numbers have been credited with smoothing out the peaks and troughs of the business cycle since the Second World War and even with the strong economic growth of the postwar era. This one miraculous figure, the GDP, apparently 'compresses the immensity of a national economy into a single data point of surpassing density'—and governments and many people believe that only this one statistic 'can really show whether things are getting better or getting worse'.

GDP measures not only record the economic life of a nation but help to determine it. They are used by governments to calculate budgets and to assess the impact of fiscal and monetary policy on an economy. They are used by politicians in campaign strategies, and by corporations for investment decisions and Wall Street takeovers. As former chairman of the US Federal Reserve Alan Greenspan acknowledges, GDP figures have 'a profound influence on markets' and 'are the basis for Federal budget projections and political rhetoric'.

So sacred is the single GDP figure to the US economy that a complex ritual has evolved around its announcement, rivalling in mystique and secrecy the selection and announcement of a new Catholic pope. Twelve times a year, chief US statistician Steven Landefeld and his team lock themselves up in Washington without phones and the internet, draw the curtains and carry out a task refined over fifty years. They have one goal in mind: to arrive at a single number through the convergence of some ten thousand data streams from recent economic activity in the US, including harvests, construction, manufacturers' shipments and retail sales. That number must not be spoken out loud. Instead, it is explained in a press release which is then photocopied many times and locked up—except for a single copy, which is delivered at the end of the day to the chairman of the US president's Council of Economic Advisers. So powerful is this figure that no one must utter it before its official revelation. Why? Because this single number is capable of rocking the world. It must not be uttered before time 'lest its premature unveiling roil the global financial markets'. Only at 8.30 am the next day is the GDP number released.

But the GDP was not designed for this purpose. It was not conceived to be the primary gauge of the economic health of a nation, it was not created to be a key tool for policymakers and investors, it was not born to govern the global financial markets. As a measure of national wellbeing, the GDP is a deeply flawed rule. Simon Kuznets himself, one of its creators, warned of the limitations of GDP measures, especially their exclusion of household production and other non-market activity, as well as the many costs of economic development. Kuznets' concerns have been reiterated ever since, most famously, as we have seen, by Senator Robert Kennedy in the speech he gave at the University of Kansas in 1968 just months before his assassination. To repeat his key points, he said:

> Gross National Product counts air pollution and cigarette advertising, and ambulances to clear our highways of carnage. It counts special locks for our doors and the jails for the people who break them. It counts the destruction of the redwood and the loss of our natural wonder in chaotic sprawl . . . Yet the gross national product does not allow for the health of our children, the quality of their education or the joy of their play. It does not include the beauty of our poetry or the strength of our marriages, the intelligence of our public debate or the integrity of our public officials . . . It measures everything, in short, except that which makes life worthwhile.

In its entirety, Kennedy's speech eloquently articulates the many failings of GDP measures. US economist

Everett Erlich said of it in 1999: 'If you were an economist with a soul, Bobby Kennedy's speech made you weep.'

New Zealand economist Marilyn Waring discovered the GDP's flaws when she became a politician and found that in her nation's economic measurements the things she most valued about her country counted for nothing: 'its pollution-free environment; its mountain streams with safe drinking water; the accessibility of national parks, walkways, beaches, lakes, kauri and beech forests; the absence of nuclear power and nuclear energy'.

The GDP measures only those things that have monetary value, only those things that are legally bought and sold. Or, in the officialese of the Australian Bureau of Statistics (ABS): 'The national accounts are a macroeconomic data set revolving around the central economic concepts of production, income, expenditure and wealth. They also comprise a monetary system, and therefore rely substantially on being able to measure the money transactions taking place between the various economic agents in a market economy.' As mentioned, they do not include unpaid work, natural resources or wilderness areas. A tree in a forest is not counted as a national asset. But when that tree is cut down and sold as timber it is measured in GDP—and only then does it contribute to economic growth as officially measured.

This is because until recently economists have assumed that natural resources are so plentiful that any loss of them is insignificant, not worth counting. They assumed that natural resources like water, soil, forests and air were free gifts of nature. And they did not consider that the natural world could be used up or worn out in the way that buildings and equipment can. But just as the nineteenth-century railway entrepreneurs had to learn that human-made capital—rails and machinery—wears out and must be depreciated, so some economists are beginning to understand that nature's capital is also subject to wear and tear and depletion.

Cambridge University's Professor Sir Partha Dasgupta is one economist who is critical of the GNP and its use to judge the progress or otherwise of nations. He argues, 'as so many economists have already done, that GNP's main weakness lies in the fact that it is insensitive to the depreciation of capital assets'. And from an environmental point of view, this is critical. GNP statistics reflect key economic flows—production, consumption, saving and investment—but they do not measure the state of the 'capital stocks' (that is, social, human and natural resources, as well as human-made capital such as buildings and equipment) from which that production is drawn. By focusing on flows, Professor Dasgupta explains, the GDP sends misleading signals to policymakers:

> Activities that maximize production in the
> short term need not preserve the capital
> stocks that are central to long-term prosperity.
> Indeed, focusing just on GDP actually creates

incentives to deplete capital stocks because the
returns are treated as income. Ultimately, not
recording the cost of reinvestments to sustain
healthy ecosystems creates and conceals
ecological liabilities.

With sustainability and climate change the big challenges of our time, we can no longer afford to leave
environmental costs off our books.

The Australian Bureau of Statistics points out that
environmental depletion 'is analogous to depreciation
of produced assets whereby the current value of the
stock of fixed assets declines from normal use', but while
depreciation of human-made assets is deducted from the
GDP to arrive at various net measures, 'No such deduc-
tion is made for natural assets when they are used up
or degraded as a result of economic activity. The net
measures thus fall short of being sustainable concepts of
income.' So says the ABS. Our national income figures
are not sustainable.

The selective economic portrait the GDP figures
paint supports economic growth at all costs. Following
the 2004 Boxing Day tsunami, a group of Sri Lankan
fishermen learnt the exacting cost of economic development as governed by the GDP. A grand plan to remake
their country—a plan which had been conceived in
the aftermath of the civil war—was carried out after
the tsunami had ruined the beaches where the fishermen lived. International organisations, including the

United States Agency for International Development (USAID), the World Bank and the Asian Development Bank, arrived to 'plot Sri Lanka's entry into the world economy', as Naomi Klein puts it. Before the makeover overseen by these organisations, the men's small-scale fishing had been their livelihood, giving them enough to feed their families. But their subsistence fishing did not contribute to economic growth as measured by the GDP figures used by organisations such as the World Bank and so it was expendable. The land where their huts had been was converted to more profitable use—in money terms—and they were left without a means to feed their children. The land on which they had lived for generations was used for GDP-enhancing international hotels and tourism, built to exploit Sri Lanka's natural beauty and its religions, which had been 'retrofitted to nourish the spiritual need of Western visitors—Buddhist monks could run meditation centres, Hindu women could perform colourful dances at hotels, Ayurvedic medical clinics could soothe aches and pains'.

Despite the development since the 1970s of several alternative measures of national prosperity, politicians have been slow to adopt them. It seems that international organisations, governments and businesses have a vested interest in GDP measures, which emphasise and even exaggerate economic growth. The Australian government's official line on environmental accounting as reported by the ABS is that:

> The economy has a complex relationship
> with the environment. The environment
> provides the raw materials and energy for
> the production of goods and services that
> support our lifestyles, but it also sustains
> damage through the activities of households
> and businesses ... While the environment
> clearly provides services to the economy, these
> are often provided at no cost or are implicit
> in the value of goods and services rather
> than in explicit transactions. Environmental
> assets are often not controlled by economic
> agents because of their physical nature, or in
> some cases are so plentiful that they have a
> zero price. For this reason, the valuation of
> environmental flows and stocks is fraught with
> conceptual and practical difficulties.

And so they are not valued at all.

Australia's environmental accounts are based on the United Nations guidelines set out in its *System of Integrated Environmental and Economic Accounting* (SEEA 2003), which gives a conceptual and classification framework for environmental accounting primarily through the development of 'satellite accounts' to be used in conjunction with—rather than integrated into—the traditional national accounts. According to the ABS, this satellite system allows 'the freedom to develop alternative concepts, classifications and measurement techniques which are different, but at the same time retain a connection back to the national accounts'. But it also means the word 'integrated' in the system's title is a misnomer—because in fact it leaves the GDP figures intact.

The UN began to develop its environmental accounting guidelines in 1992, when it recommended that the GDP and other traditional systems of national income measurement include supplementary environmental and social information. Most countries have since attempted to expand their national accounts to include such satellite accounts. The United States published its first environmental satellite accounts in 1994, which adjusted the GDP for the depletion of oil and other non-renewable resources. But the figures with their downgraded view of US wealth proved so controversial and so politically explosive that Congress shut down the programme almost the moment the revised numbers were published. Everett Erlich highlights the Orwellian nature of this move when he says that by putting a stop to the US environmental accounts, 'Congress made thinking about a Green GDP a thought crime'.

The current state of environmental accounting in Australia is compromised, to say the least. Australia records the value only of environmental assets that fall within a so-called 'asset boundary'—which includes only those natural assets which have an identifiable owner who can 'derive an economic benefit from the use of the asset'. Within the asset boundary are subsoil assets (or mineral deposits), land, forests, water and fish stocks in open seas under the control of an economic agent (which is often the government). But it does not include the atmosphere or ecosystems that do not have an identifiable owner who benefits economically from their use. As the ABS makes clear: 'This is not to suggest that these assets are of no value. On the contrary, many of them are essential to life itself. However, even if they fell within the definition of an economic asset, the valuation techniques available to measure such assets tend to be arbitrary and controversial.' As most accounting is, when examined closely. Here we begin to see the limits of so-called environmental accounting.

Although it pays lip service to environmental accounts, in 2006 the ABS concluded that 'work on the valuation of environmental damage (externalities associated with human and economic activity) is an undeveloped field of research and it is unlikely that the ABS will have the capacity to make advances in this area in the foreseeable future'. The key word here is 'externalities', which veils a multitude of sins. In economics an externality is a cost, but one not transferred through prices and therefore not accounted for. The pollution of waterways or the atmosphere by factories, for example, is an externality.

Despite the almost universal resistance to accounting for nature, many economists are now beginning to acknowledge the environment's contribution to economic life—for example, the value of the goods and services it provides for the market economy through its production of raw materials, water purification, waste decomposition, soil maintenance, pollination, pest control, and the regulation of local and global climates. In just one small example, according to Worldwatch Institute senior researcher Janet Abramovitz, 'Honeybee pollination activity is 60 to 100 times more valuable than the honey they produce. The value of wild blueberry bees is so great, with each one pollinating four to five gallons of blueberries in its life, that farmers view them as "flying $50 bills".' These services are not included in the GDP because they are believed to be free. But as Abramovitz says, 'nature's services are not, in fact, free, and the future will bear the hidden costs of losing them'.

Environmental accounting is urgently needed at a national level not only for the survival of the environment itself, but also for its potential impact on poverty. The current GDP national accounting system privileges developed economies with human-made capital over nations with vast natural assets. Professor Dasgupta is a passionate advocate of the poverty-reducing potential of national environmental accounting. He argues that 'poverty will only be made history when nature enters economic calculations in the same way as do buildings, machines, roads and for example software'. According to Dasgupta, this will involve creating markets that give real and long-lasting value to the goods and services nature provides, rather than treating them as free and limitless, as do traditional measures such as the GDP.

Nature's services include carbon absorption by forests, the coastal defence (from erosion, storm damage and flooding) provided by coral reefs, the pollution-filtering potential of wetlands and the nutrient recycling carried out by the soil. Under current GDP measures, countries that cut down forests for timber exports, dynamite their reefs for fish, pollute and degrade their soil for intensive agriculture, and allow farms and factories to contaminate their waterways appear to be getting richer in the short term. In fact, they are using up their natural capital. Dasgupta gives the example of India:

> On the basis of traditional measures, like
> GDP, the region has been getting richer
> since the 1970s but in reality wealth per
> capita has actually declined. This is because,
> relative to population growth, investments
> in manufactured capital, knowledge, skills
> and health, and improvements in institutions
> were not sufficient to compensate for the
> depreciation of natural capital.

The potential consequences of our ignorance of nature are alarming, both for us and for future generations. Former Executive Director of the United Nations Environment Programme, Klaus Toepfer, outlines the implications of our current economic models:

> By continually depleting and damaging [nature]
> and without investment in the running,
> maintenance and management costs, the

Earth's life support can suddenly and abruptly
fade or switch to become less productive and
predictable. I believe we are slowly winning
this political and economic argument but not
fast enough. So we must hurry up otherwise all
six billion of us will eventually be scratching
around trying to survive.

The findings of the UN-supported Millennium Ecosystem Assessment, first published in 2005, make clear
just how much we are damaging the planet: some 60 per
cent of the earth's ecosystem services are being degraded
by human activities. Dasgupta says the Millennium
Ecosystem Assessment has given a powerful message to
economists about the urgency of valuing natural assets:
'estimating shadow prices of such vital assets as local
and global ecosystems and the services they offer is now
of central importance'.

Although most of the goods and services provided by
ecosystems have as yet little or no market value, some
have been valued by the Millennium Ecosystem Assessment, which found that their estimated monetary values
far exceed their current dollar value in the market economy. For example, it calculated that an intact wetland
in Canada is worth US$6000 a hectare compared with
US$2000 a hectare for one cleared for intensive agri-
culture. Intact tropical mangroves—coastal ecosystems
which serve as nurseries for fish, natural pollution fil-
ters and coastal defences—are worth around US$1000

a hectare. Cleared for shrimp farms, the value falls to around US$200 a hectare. The Muthurajawela Marsh, a coastal bog of over 3000 hectares in Sri Lanka, is worth an estimated US$5 million a year for its services, which include local flood control.

And forests are worth much more alive than when they are cut down for timber. The carbon storage, or sequestration, potential of forests ranges between US$360 and US$2200 per hectare, far more than their worth when cleared for grazing or crops. When the price of carbon is more than US$30 a ton, it is more cost effective to conserve forests than to clear them. Tropical forests are worth some US$60 billion a year as a result of their carbon removal activities alone. But these forests, found in countries like Indonesia and the Democratic Republic of the Congo, are currently valued only for their timber, not for their even more valuable carbon sequestration services. The burning of 10 million hectares of Indonesian forests in the late 1990s cost an estimated US$9 billion, a figure which includes the costs of rising health care and the fall in tourism. Studies from Algeria, Italy, Portugal, Syria and Tunisia estimate the value of forests for timber and fuelwood is less than a third of that of intact forests for watershed protection, recreation and the absorption of greenhouse gases. Environmental destruction also exacerbates the spread of disease: studies in the Amazon have shown that for every 1 per cent increase in deforestation, there is an 8 per cent increase in the number of malaria-carrying mosquitoes.

A 2003 project in New York City called Neighborhood Tree Survey provides a telling example of the way the pricing of nature can affect our attitudes and behaviour towards it. The survey calculated the value in dollars of 322 trees in New York City based on the amount the city would have to pay to replace each tree. Their total value was US$1,038,458, with an average value of US$3225 per tree. The most expensive tree? A 214-year-old tulip tree on Staten Island, worth US$23,069. The cheapest was a six-year-old ginkgo in the South Bronx, valued at US$54. The organisers hoped that putting price tags on trees would 'help people realize the real value of street trees'.

The New York Parks Department's chief of forestry and horticulture said of the experiment: 'People always knew there was some vague benefit to trees, but you could never quantify it. But once you have the methodology to equate trees with dollars, now you're talking. It's no longer about hugging trees because they're good, but because you have hard data in a language more effective in the public dialogue.' In our global market economy, it seems money speaks louder than nature. According to the executive director of American Forests, Deborah Gangloff, the ecological value of America's urban forests is worth US$4 billion annually, in terms of clean air and water. They also cool cities, buffer rainstorms and look beautiful.

In 2008, the Living Planet Survey initiated by the World Wildlife Fund found that we are running up a planet-wide 'ecological debt' of US$4 trillion to US$4.5 trillion every year. These figures happen to be twice—two times!—the amount of the estimated losses suffered by the world's financial institutions from the 2008 global financial crisis. The authors of the report said 'the possibility of financial recession pales in comparison to the looming ecological credit crunch'—and called for politicians to respond to the environmental crisis with the same urgency and magnitude as their multi-billion-dollar rescue plan for the failed financial system.

Perhaps their call did not fall on deaf ears. Recently the GDP as traditionally measured has been actively challenged by several world leaders and international bodies like the OECD. It seems that at last, after all the evidence of the shortcomings of economic growth as a measure of national prosperity and the decades-long criticisms of GDP accounting, the 2008 financial collapse and the increasingly apparent environmental crisis have together created some political momentum for the radical revision of our methods of national accounting.

In 2009 France's President Nicolas Sarkozy questioned the GDP as a measure of national wellbeing. As he noted, 'the global economic crisis and fluctuating commodity prices of recent years have laid bare both the deficiencies of our accounting structures and our dependence on finite and fragile natural systems'. Feeling the pressure of the competing demands made upon him for economic growth *and* environmental protection,

Sarkozy called on economist and Nobel laureate Joseph Stiglitz. As Stiglitz recounts, Sarkozy's dilemma is that he 'is told to maximize GDP but he also knows as a good politician that what people care about are things like pollution and many other dimensions to the quality of life. Those dimensions aren't well captured in GDP . . . And so he sort of said, Can't you in some way resolve this tension by constructing measures that don't pose these dichotomies?' Stiglitz believes he can.

In response, Sarkozy established a commission to consider alternatives to the GDP, recruiting Stiglitz, as well as another Nobel laureate, economist Amartya Sen, and economist Jean-Paul Fitoussi to 'tear apart the GDP' as they saw fit. The Stiglitz-Sen-Fitoussi Commission released its report in September 2009, making suggestions for measuring the progress of nations in ways better suited to the twenty-first century. The commission endorsed both main criticisms of the GDP, arguing that 'the economic measure itself should be fixed to better represent individuals' circumstances today, and every country should also apply other indicators to capture what is happening economically, socially and environmentally'. It recommended using at least seven different measures to assess national quality of life: health, education, environment, employment, material wellbeing, interpersonal connectedness and political engagement. It also recommended measuring equity, and economic and environmental sustainability. Stiglitz believes that the 2008 global financial crisis requires us to rethink our social contract. As he says, 'We should also, in the aftermath of an extraordinary economic collapse, talk about what the goals of a society really are.'

The recommendations of the Stiglitz-Sen-Fitoussi Commission have so far been debated by the European Union and the OECD. The head of Italy's national statistics agency, Enrico Giovanni, thinks this is, at least, a start. He says: 'The good news, I think, is that at the international level there are signs that something is changing.'

Economist Paul Ormerod believes the revision of national accounting methods is important not so much for the figures which might emerge from any amended system as for the sake of providing a catalyst to spur governments to alter the emphasis of their policies. He argues that 'the inclusion of more non-market factors in the national accounts, such as the cost of pollution or the cost of traffic congestion, would encourage governments to take these problems more seriously and try to do something about them'. Journalist Jon Gertner concurs with this view. Any attempt to bring non-market factors within the ambit of national accounts would have the effect of pricing the trees of New York City. It would provide hard data in a language which carries more weight in public debate in capitalist societies than moral abstractions such as 'goodness': the language of money. Or, as Gertner puts it, in a green accounting context, 'a heightened focus on environmental indicators, for starters, could give environmental legislation far greater urgency'.

Amartya Sen has arrived at a similarly pragmatic view. Sen's involvement with alternate approaches to national accounting goes back to 1990, when he formulated the Human Development Index (HDI) with friend and colleague Mahbub ul Haq. The HDI incorporates into a nation's accounts GDP modified by education and health. Sen and Haq met at Cambridge University in 1953, where they found they shared an interest in national development and agreed that it was wrong to equate development with economic growth. Haq began to consider measures other than the GDP, mostly in health and education, which he believed might lead to government policies that would massively improve life in countries like his native Pakistan even without large increases in the GDP.

Some years after they graduated, Haq asked Sen to help him construct the HDI. Sen says he immediately 'recoiled' at the idea. 'I told Mahbub that it's vulgar to capture in one number an extremely complex story, just as GDP is vulgar. And he called me back and said: "Amartya, you're exactly right. What I want you to do is produce an index as vulgar as GDP but more relevant to our own lives." ' Sen eventually saw 'the wisdom of Haq's pragmatism' and agreed to work on the HDI. But since they formulated the HDI in 1990, climate change has become far more evident and the need to address it with new environmental accounting measures is more pressing, hence Sen's willing involvement in Sarkozy's commission.

And in March 2008, at long last—forty years after his speech questioning GDP accounting—Robert Kennedy's questions were taken up by the US government in Washington. A United States Senate Committee discussed the GDP's failure to measure environmental damage, poverty, income inequality, health and the quality of life, as well as the danger of using the GDP to express national wellbeing. At the time of the Senate hearing, there was no US legislation to accommodate a possible revision to US national accounting. But two years later, on 23 March 2010, President Barack Obama signed into law the Patient Protection and Affordable Care Act which contains one small section—section 5605—which requires that Congress help fund and oversee the creation of a new 'key national indicators system'. The 'State of the USA', a set of measurements independently created by its president and CEO Chris Hoenig, will become that system. Founded as a tax-exempt organisation in 2007, the State of the USA contains several hundred new measures—for health, education, ageing, families and children, crime and justice, arts and culture, the environment, the economy—which will be freely accessible online. Hoenig calls the GDP 'an artefact of a world before the Web' and believes his online indicators are more suited in form and content to the new millennium. He hopes that with easy access to these key indicators Americans might be able to 'shift the debate from opinions to more evidence-based discussions' and make the United States the first country in the world whose population enjoys 'a shared, quantitative frame of reference'.

From an environmental perspective, the main accounting challenge we face is in defining, quantifying and valuing natural capital. With this in mind, the European Union's European Environment Agency (EEA) and its partners have been developing ways of recording the ecosystem's contribution to national welfare. Its 'ecosystem accounts' include both physical and monetary accounts of stocks (that is, records of the actual holdings of the natural environment as well as their monetary value), material and energy flows, and services. Its basic approach is not so different from that of the NYC Neighborhood Tree Survey. It involves working out the level of investments needed to ensure that ecosystems continue to provide the same level of services. The EEA is also preparing land, carbon and water accounts to show their physical changes within Europe and the economic impact of such changes.

The EEA believes it is better to create these simplified ecosystem accounts now than to wait until a comprehensive approach is developed. As it points out, that is exactly how the UN System of National Accounts—which is now seen as gospel—was created. The SNA began in 1953 under Richard Stone as a basic 56-page document and is now a comprehensive 750 pages. 'The message is clear: start simple.'

Economist Pavan Sukhdev, the author of the United Nation's 2010 biodiversity report *Global Biodiversity*

Outlook 3, says that unless we value the goods and services of the natural world and factor them into the global economic system, we will continue to destroy the environment and make it less resistant to shocks, at the risk of life and livelihoods. He believes the changes required will entail a 'wholesale revolution' in the way we do business, consume, and think about our lives. The UN biodiversity report advocates 'massive changes to the way the global economy is run so that it factors in the value of the natural world'. It argues that communities should be paid to conserve nature rather than for using it. Corporations must be strictly limited in what they can take from the environment. And business and governments must account for their use of natural and human capital alongside their financial results. The world it envisions is regulated by an accounting system made for the twenty-first century and for the future of human life on earth.

In February 2011, Sukhdev's *Green Economy Report*, part of his work with the United Nations Environment Programme, was launched with the headline 'How two per cent of global GDP can trigger green growth and fight poverty'. It outlines how investing 2 per cent of global GDP, or around US$1.3 trillion a year, in ten key sectors would convert the world's 'brown' economy into a 'green' economy, and challenges the prevailing belief that there needs to be a trade-off between economic growth and environmental investments.

The *Green Economy Report* was part of the UN's preparation for 'Rio+20', or 'Earth Summit 2012', the UN's

Conference on Sustainable Development held in Rio de Janeiro in June 2012. The Earth Summit had two major focuses—the green economy in the context of sustainable development and poverty eradication, and the creation of an institutional framework for sustainable development—and was supported by nations around the world, including the leaders of the G20, the world's twenty largest developed and emerging economies. It seems that at last the momentum is with those who for so many decades have despaired over GDP measures and sought their revision.

Through the way it values—or does not—the finite resources of our planet, double entry now has the potential to make or break life on the earth. We can continue to ignore the free gifts of nature in the accounts of our nations and corporations, and thereby continue to ruin the planet. Or we can begin to account for nature and make it thrive again. If numbers and money are the only language spoken in the global capitalist economy, then this is the language we must use. Accountants, remodelled as eco-accountants, can play a central role in this conversation—and it is for this reason that Jonathan Watts wrote in 2010 that they may be the one last hope for life on earth. As he also pointed out, done badly, eco-accounting will mean the natural world is further 'commodified, priced, sliced and sold to the highest bidder'. But done well, it could reframe our values and transform the capitalist world in ways we are yet to imagine.

EPILOGUE

... once we allow ourselves to be disobedient to
the test of an accountant's profit, we have begun to
change our civilisation ...

JOHN MAYNARD KEYNES, 1933

The old way of measuring value is becoming
irrelevant.

AL GORE, 2006

THE CORPORATE FORM AND ITS LANGUAGE—ACCOUNT-
ing—have exacted social and environmental
costs for which we have not only failed to pay, but
which we have also failed to recognise. Until now. The
thirteenth-century Venetian system of double-entry
bookkeeping codified by Luca Pacioli in 1494 has morphed into an exacting global calculus and created a
culture that makes possible reasoning which generates
ruthless decisions such as the following infamous life–
death choice. This is the cost-benefit analysis of the
Ford Motor Company from 1977, weighing the relative
merits of adding or not adding a safety device to its

Pinto car, an analysis which entailed assessing the 'cost of safety parts versus the cost of lives lost', where the 'cost of lives lost' is the dollar value of men, women and children potentially killed in the unsafe vehicles. An internal company memorandum estimated that 'if the Pinto was sold without the $11 safety feature, 2100 cars would burn every year, 180 people would be hurt but survive, and another 180 would burn to death'. Ford made the following analysis:

Benefits	*Costs*
money saved by a safer car:	money spent on safety device:
180 deaths × $200,000	11 million cars × $11 per part
+ 180 injuries × $67,000	+ 1.5 million trucks × $11
+ 2100 vehicles × $700	
= $49.5 million	= $137.5 million

Clearly the costs of the safety device far exceed its benefits. In accounting terms. And so naturally Ford decided not to spend money on the safety feature, based on the inexorable logic of these two simple numerical equations. This is a classic example of accounting-driven cost-benefit analysis. According to the journalist who broke the story, Mark Dowie, between 1971, when the Pinto was introduced, and 1977, when the magazine *Mother Jones* printed his analysis of the case, at least five hundred people burnt to death in Pinto crashes.

Our modern urge to measure everything dates back to the late Middle Ages when a 'radical change of perception' took place in which mathematics, Venetian bookkeeping and Luca Pacioli played a key role. Historian Alfred W. Crosby explains this 'radical change':

> In practical terms the new approach was simply this: reduce what you are trying to think about to the minimum required by its definition; visualise it on paper, or at least in your mind, be it the fluctuation of wool prices at the Champagne fairs or the course of Mars through the heavens, and divide it, either in fact or in imagination, into equal quanta. Then you can measure it, that is, count the quanta.

And once you can measure something, then you have a quantitative or numerical representation of your subject which you can manipulate and experiment with, no matter how great its errors or omissions. Such data can acquire an apparent independence from its human creators and, when fed into a twenty-first-century computer model, an authority that appears irrefutable. 'It can do for you what verbal representation rarely does: contradict your fondest wishes and elbow you on to more efficacious speculation.'

For better or worse, accounting is our way of measuring the way we use all the precious resources of this planet, human, natural and synthetic. Accounting is fundamental to the functioning and development of twenty-first-century societies. And the way we measure our resources—or don't measure them—determines how we value the earth and consequently influences the way we behave. As Joseph Stiglitz says: 'What we measure affects what we do, and better measurement will lead to better decisions, or at least different decisions.'

And yet, as we have seen, despite their enormous significance and power to shape life on earth, accounting's measures are fundamentally arbitrary and go largely unchallenged. As long ago as 1978, Professor Anthony Hopwood noted accounting's mostly unquestioned role in shaping society. He said:

> there are few, if any, signs of interest in studies
> which question the formal roles served by
> accounting information, the negotiated and
> political nature of technical accounting
> solutions and the way in which design options
> are constrained and shaped. For such studies
> *of* accounting rather than *in* accounting, where
> accountancy itself is regarded as a problematic,
> organisational and social process influenced
> by, and in turn influencing many vital elements
> of the wider context in which it operates, are
> quite obviously capable of challenging the
> status quo by providing a basis on which to
> question what has not been questioned and
> what some would prefer not to be questioned.

In an era of international capital, when our wealth

is more than ever tied up in its fortunes, and at a time when corporations, governments and financial institutions are demonstrating their fallibility on a global scale, it is essential that we are aware of the somewhat arbitrary laws of account that govern them—especially because it is in the labyrinthine workings of our accounting systems that value itself is assigned. It seems that if we want to bring our infinitely voracious consumerism into line with the resources of our finite planet, we must consider giving our planet a value that the market can recognise and account for, assign a monetary value to the oceans, air, forests, rivers, wildernesses. As the global economy continues to collapse around us, yet to remake itself, and the earth's resources are increasingly threatened with exhaustion, this would seem to be one of our key economic and ethical challenges for the twenty-first century. In one way or another, this century will be the one in which we learn to account for our planet. Because unless we start accounting for our transactions with the earth, we will bankrupt it for all future human habitation.

ACKNOWLEDGEMENTS

My massive thanks go to the following people:

To Michael Hill, who encouraged me to write this book when it was just an idea and who supported me the whole way, which was long.

To Jane Palfreyman, a great friend and the best publisher a writer could hope for. For all her continuing support, enthusiasm, intelligence and wit.

To Clara Finlay, my brilliant editor, for her in-house organisational magic as well as her copyedit which showed me the way. Far from being an invisible mender, she was my stylist.

To Ali Lavau for her astute, enthusiastic and gently critical (in the best possible way) structural edit. She helped me to understand how to shape this apparently boundless material.

To Aziza Kuypers for her eagle-eyed proofreading that went way beyond proofreading. Her questions prompted me to think more deeply at several key moments in the manuscript.

I was extremely fortunate in my publisher and three editors.

To publisher Patrick Gallagher for his ongoing support and martinis.

To Peter Long for his beautiful internal design and a cover which captures the arc of my book in one image.

To Giovanni Fazzini at the Biblioteca Nazionale Marciana in Venice, who gave me invaluable help with accessing dozens of articles and books which shed light on the work of Luca Pacioli, the Scuola di Rialto and Venetian mathematics.

To my wonderful hosts at the Casa Mila in Sansepolcro, Val and Colin Stevens, who treated me like family. And to Val especially for activating her Sansepolcro networks on my behalf to gain me entrance to places I would either not have known about or not have been allowed access to, such as the Sansepolcro Biblioteca Comunale. And to the librarians at that library, for letting me look at the 1494 edition of the *Summa de arithmetica, geometria, proportione et proportionalità* and *De divina proportione*.

To Jackson and Scarlet Hill, for being such wonderful company, for making me laugh (mostly at myself, essential when writing about monks and mathematics), and for enduring my long absences, either at my desk or in my head, over the last three years.

To Gaby Naher, a great friend whose regular emails and morning coffee dates were often the only contact I had with the outside world while I wrote this book.

And once more, to my family and friends for still talking to me despite the fact that I spent the last three years locked away in my study writing about a monk.

NOTES

Direct quotes are in quote marks; indirect references are indicated in italics.

Preface

p. 4 'By rights, by logic . . .'   John Lanchester, 'It's finished', *London Review of Books*, 28 May 2009.

p. 9 'So it has come to this . . .'   Jonathan Watts, 'Are accountants the last hope for the world's ecosystems?', *Guardian*, 28 October 2010.

Chapter 1

p. 10 'Anodyne Pills for Breachy . . .'   Joel Achenbach, 'All the president's pennies: Washington, the meticulous businessman', *Sydney Morning Herald*, 17–18 October 2009.

p. 11 'statement of moneys . . .'   *Oxford English Dictionary*, Clarendon Press, Oxford, 1989.

p. 13 *Mattessich suggested that . . .*   John Richard Edwards and Stephen P. Walker (eds), *The Routledge Companion to Accounting History*, Routledge, Abingdon, Oxon, 2009, p. 96.

p. 14 'but because it encouraged . . .'   Richard Brown, *A History of Accounting and Accountants*, T.C. & E.C. Jack, Edinburgh, 1905, p. 17.

p. 14 'If the merchant has given . . .'   Ibid, p. 24.

p. 15 *If they failed to do so . . .*   Alvaro Martinelli, 'Notes on the origin of double-entry bookkeeping', *Abacus*, vol. 13, issue 1, 1977, pp. 3–27, p. 15.

p. 16 'make an annual statement of all our income...' www.le.ac. uk/hi/polyptyques/capitulare/site.html, University of Leicester, School of Historical Studies, 'Carolingian Polyptyques', accessed 23 March 2009.

p. 17 'That Jerusalem was won...' A.C. Littleton, *Accounting Evolution to 1900*, Russell & Russell, New York, 1966, p. 17.

p. 18 'There, following my introduction...' Fibonacci, *Liber abaci*, Springer Publishing, New York, 2002, p. 3.

p. 20 *the six essential features of double-entry bookkeeping...* G.A. Lee, 'Farolfi Ledger 1299–1300', *The Development of Double Entry: Selected essays*, Christopher W. Nobes (ed.), Garland Publishing Inc., New York, 1984.

p. 22 'We would remark that the *Banias*...' *AccountAble*, issue 6, October–December 2005.

p. 22 *Although there is very little surviving...* B.M. Lall Nigam, 'Bahi-Khata: The pre-Pacioli Indian double-entry system of bookkeeping', *Abacus*, vol. 22, no. 2, pp. 148–61.

p. 23 'only by buying the services...' Alfred W. Crosby, *The Measure of Reality: Quantification and western society, 1250–1600*, Cambridge University Press, Cambridge, 1997, p. 55.

p. 23 *One of these new counting men...* The account of Datini is taken from Iris Origo's excellent study of his life and times, *The Merchant of Prato: Francesco di Marco Datini*, Jonathan Cape, London, 1957.

CHAPTER 2

p. 30 'As the Pope...' Niccolò Machiavelli, *The Historical, Political and Diplomatic Writings*, Book 6, J.R. Osgood & Co., Boston, 1882.

p. 35 'The good Christian should...' Frank J. Swetz, *Capitalism and Arithmetic: The new math of the fifteenth century*, Open Court, La Salle, 1987, p. 284.

p. 37 'God made the sun so that...' Bertrand Russell, *A History of Western Philosophy*, Unwin Paperbacks, London, 1984, p. 157.

p. 37 'undesirable for a philosopher ...' Ibid., p. 64.

p. 38 *The mathematics taught, however, was basic ...* Ibid., p. 136.

p. 38 'There is a fish that ...' This example comes from Piero della Francesca's *Trattato d'abaco*, c. 1450.

p. 41 *By 1338 Florence had six ...* Swetz, op. cit., p. 283.

p. 43 'we have always customarily ...' James R. Banker, *The Culture of San Sepolcro during the Youth of Piero della Francesca*, University of Michigan Press, Ann Arbor, 2003, p. 63.

p. 45 'And in this treatise I promise to give you a full knowledge ...' R. Emmett Taylor, *No Royal Road: Luca Pacioli and his times*, Arno Press, New York, 1980, p. 28.

p. 46 'The man who should ...' Giorgio Vasari, *The Lives of the Artists*, Oxford University Press, New York, 1998, p. 163.

p. 47 'who awakened in Pacioli a desire to ...' Ibid., p. 163.

p. 47 *Among the scraps of evidence ...* Basil S. Yamey, *Art and Accounting*, Yale University Press, New Haven, 1989.

CHAPTER 3

p. 49 'This damp expanse, speckled with islets ...' Jan Morris, *Venice*, Faber & Faber, London, 1993, p. 244.

p. 50 'the moneys of our dominion ...' Frederic C. Lane and Reinhold C. Mueller, *Money and Banking in Medieval and Renaissance Venice*, The Johns Hopkins University Press, Baltimore, 1985, p. xiii.

p. 51 'O sea, we wed ...' Ibid., p. 287.

p. 52 *The busy life of one Venetian merchant ...* This account is drawn from Edward Peragallo, 'The ledger of Jachomo Badoer: Constantinople September 2, 1436 to February 26, 1440', *The Accounting Review*, vol. 52, no. 4, October 1977, pp. 881–92.

p. 57 'illustrious pupils, the brothers ...' Taylor, op. cit., p. 49.

p. 60 'the root of all things ...' Fernand Braudel, *Civilization and Capitalism, 15th–18th Century*, William Collins Sons & Co. Ltd, London, 1982.

p. 65 'If I do not seem to have treated these . . .'   Taylor, op. cit., p. 129.

p. 71 'almost missionary faith . . .'   Paul Lawrence Rose, *The Italian Renaissance of Mathematics: Studies on humanists and mathematicians from Petrarch to Galileo*, Librarie Droz, Geneva, 1975, p. 293.

p. 72 'industry in the workshop . . .'   Taylor, op. cit., p. 179.

p. 72 'this volume of mine possible . . .'   Ibid., p. 188.

p. 72 'each and every man . . .'   Ibid., p. 190.

p. 73 'Why, the citadels of states . . .'   Ibid., p. 193.

p. 74 'the arrangement of the work . . .'   Ibid., p. 201.

p. 74 *The* Summa *is divided into two volumes . . .*   A. Sangster, G.N. Stoner and P. McCarthy, 'The market for Luca Pacioli's *Summa Arithmetica*', *The Accounting Historians Journal*, vol. 35, June 2008, pp. 111–34.

p. 76 *The* Summa *moves from using algebra . . .*   Albrecht Heeffer, 'From problem solving to argumentation, Pacioli's appropriation of Abbacus Algebra', Centre for Logic and Philosophy of Science, Ghent University, http://logica.ugent.be/centrum.

p. 78 *Priced at 119 soldi . . .*   Sangster et al., op. cit., pp. 111–34.

p. 79 'captures one of the greatest moments . . .'   The discussion of Luca Pacioli's portrait is taken from Nick Mackinnon, 'The portrait of Fra Luca Pacioli', *The Mathematical Gazette*, vol. 2, 1993, pp. 130–219.

p. 80 'took with him a lyre . . .'   For the stories on Leonardo I draw from Charles Nicholl's excellent biography *Leonardo da Vinci: The flights of the mind*, Penguin, London, 2004, unless otherwise indicated.

p. 81 'of a fine person . . .'   Martin Kemp, *Leonardo*, Oxford University Press, Oxford, 2004, p. 44.

p. 82 'the subtlest investigation . . .'   Kim H. Veltman, *Studies on Leonardo da Vinci I: Linear perspective and the visual dimensions of science and art*, Deutscher Kunstverlag, Munich, 1986, p. 62.

p. 83 'it will appear to be . . .'   Lucy McDonald, 'And that's Renaissance magic', *Guardian*, 10 April 2007.

p. 84 'When they especially disdain . . .' Desiderius Erasmus, *In Praise of Folly*, Reeves and Turner, London, 1876, p. 75.

p. 86 'everyone who loves . . .'   Taylor, op. cit., p. 255.

p. 86 'no old women's tales . . .'   Ibid., p. 258.

p. 88 'according to what we understand . . .'   Ibid., p. 365.

p. 89 'The science of mathematics, . . .'   Ibid, p. 320.

Chapter 4

p. 92 'special treatise . . .'   John B. Geijsbeek, *Ancient Double-Entry Bookkeeping: Luca Pacioli's treatise*, 1914, reprinted by Nihon Shoseki Ltd, Osaka, 1975, p. 15.

p. 92 'nothing else than the . . .'   Ibid., p. 15.

p. 93 'all about his business . . .'   Ibid.

p. 93 'This treatise will adopt . . .'   Ibid.

p. 93 'All the creditors must appear . . .'   Ibid.

p. 94 'Although one cannot write . . .'   Ibid.

p. 94 'is very essential to . . .'   Ibid.

p. 95 'on the sea, on land . . .'   Ibid, p. 19.

p. 97 'For, if he does not . . .'   Ibid, p. 17.

p. 97 'to make a lawful . . .'   Ibid.

p. 98 'must always put down . . .'   Ibid.

p. 98 'so many rooms . . .'   Ibid., p. 19.

p. 98 'so that you can easily . . .'   Ibid.

p. 99 'a book in which . . .'   Ibid.

p. 100 'that those are the books . . .'   Ibid., p. 21.

p. 102 Per *pepper* // A *capital* . . .   Ibid., p. 23.

p. 104 'must always have in mind . . .'   Ibid., p. 25.

p. 104 'you shall make two different entries . . .'   Ibid.

p. 104 'the merchant must have a much . . .'   Ibid.

p. 105 'On this day we have . . .'   Ibid., p. 27.

p. 106 'you must never make a credit entry . . .'   Ibid.

p. 107 'good written evidence as to debits . . .'   Ibid., p. 29.

p. 107 'in these offices they . . .'   Ibid.

p. 108 'And justly the glorious republic of Venice . . .'   Ibid.

p. 108 'well-known and peculiar mercantile . . .'   Ibid.

p. 109 'which you can find nowadays in Venice . . .'   Ibid., p. 31.

p. 109 'originate from overs or shorts in the debits and credits . . .'   Ibid.

p. 110 'you will see at a glance . . .'   Ibid.

p. 111 'it is always good to close . . .'   Ibid., p. 33.

p. 112 'you will be able to know what . . .'   Ibid.

p. 112 'at the beginning of your management . . .'   Ibid.

p. 113 'for, if you are not a good bookkeeper . . .'   Ibid., p. 35.

CHAPTER 5

p. 116 'was neither Latin nor the vernacular . . .'   Elizabeth L. Eisenstein, *The Printing Press as an Agent of Change*, Cambridge University Press, Cambridge, 1979, p. 531.

p. 116 'provide the most plausible . . .'   Ibid., p. 701.

p. 117 *It turns out that what Leon Battista Alberti . . .*   J.V. Field, *Piero della Francesca: A mathematician's art*, Yale University Press, New Haven, 2005, p. 294.

p. 118 'The *Ledger* is the *Waste-book . . .*'   Bruce G. Carruthers and Wendy Nelson Espeland, 'Accounting for rationality: Double-entry bookkeeping and the rhetoric of economic rationality', *American Journal of Sociology*, vol. 97, no. 1, July 1991, pp. 31–69, p. 58.

p. 119 *The fact that Pacioli was . . .*   Geijsbeek, op. cit., p. 11.

p. 120 'merchants are better informed . . .'   Brown, op. cit., p. 137.

p. 121 'alas, the small love . . .'   Ibid., p. 153.

p. 122 'Q: Why make you Cash Debtor? . . .'   Littleton, op. cit., p. 50.

p. 122 'First I will book . . .'   Ibid., p. 52.

p. 124 'This way of accounting . . .'   Basil Yamey, *Essays on the History of Accounting*, Arno Press, New York, 1978, p. 142.

p. 124 'it behoveth him . . .'   Ibid.

p. 125 'This phrase ["he has not kept true . . ."]' Carruthers and Espeland, op. cit., p. 42.

p. 126 'Also excellent use . . .' Ibid., p. 59.

p. 127 'Book-keeping by Double Entry . . .' Yamey, *Essays on the History of Accounting*, op. cit., p. 141.

p. 128 'very impartially . . .' Daniel Defoe, *Robinson Crusoe*, Penguin, Ringwood, 1985, p. 83.

p. 128 'tho' the exactest book-keeping . . .' Daniel Defoe, *The Complete English Tradesman*, 1725–27, www.online-literature.com/defoe/english-tradesman/20.

p. 129 'At that time, you had no . . .' Johann Wolfgang von Goethe, *Wilhelm Meister's Apprenticeship*, Bell & Daldy, London, 1867, p. 27.

CHAPTER 6

p. 134 *The passions it inspired . . .* Yamey, *Essays on the History of Accounting*, op. cit., p. 137.

p. 134 'For every debit there must . . .' Brown, op. cit., p. 160.

p. 135 'the false prophet had . . .' Yamey, *Essays on the History of Accounting*, op. cit., p. 321.

p. 137 'the perpetual restless ambition . . .' Thomas K. McCraw, *Creating Modern Capitalism: How entrepreneurs, companies, and countries triumphed in three industrial revolutions*, Harvard University Press, Harvard, 1995, p. 40.

p. 137 'no getting to the door for Coaches . . .' Ibid., p. 45.

p. 137 'classic symptoms of uncontrolled . . .' Robin Reilly, *Josiah Wedgwood*, Thames & Hudson, London, 1994, p. 112.

p. 138 'Consider that these expences move like clockwork . . .' Ibid., p. 46.

p. 139 *Two books on account-keeping for factories . . .* The following discussion of the joint stock company draws on Littleton, op. cit., p. 325.

p. 141 *But in the case of railways . . .* Jolyon Jenkins, 'A brief history of double-entry bookkeeping', BBC podcast March 2010. The following discussion of railways draws on Jenkins.

p. 142 'Indeed, it might be claimed . . .' Yamey, *Essays on the History of Accounting*, op. cit., p. 105.

p. 143 *Ironically, if Hudson and . . .* Jenkins, op. cit.

p. 143 'It is by the Government . . .' Edwards and Walker, op. cit., p. 111.

p. 145 'did more than anything . . .' Littleton, op. cit., p. 280.

p. 147 'the law of England . . .' Ibid., p. 249.

p. 148 'no ship arrives to signal . . .' Carruthers and Espeland, op. cit., p. 46.

p. 150 'The whole affairs in bankruptcy . . .' Littleton, op. cit., p. 282.

p. 150 'could give no proper . . .' Brown, op. cit., p. 234.

p. 150 'If my nephew is steady . . .' Ibid., p. 197.

p. 151 'It is certainly more varied . . .' Ibid., p. 316.

p. 152 'That the profession of Accountants . . .' Ibid., p. 207.

p. 153 *The new institute chose the prominent . . .* Edwards and Walker, op. cit., p. 526.

p. 155 *the New York Light Company . . .* Gary Giroux, 'Accounting History Page', http://acct.tamu.edu/giroux/history.html, A Short History of Accounting, accessed 6 August 2009, p. 2.

p. 155 'Here for the first time since . . .' Ibid.

p. 156 *With its vast resources . . .* Jenkins, op. cit.

p. 156 *The Institute of Accountants and Bookkeepers . . .* Edwards and Walker, op. cit., p. 259.

p. 157 'the virtue, experience and . . .' Ibid., p. 260.

p. 157 'they who wish to obtain . . .' Geijsbeek, op. cit., p. 5.

p. 158 'the late claimant . . .' Littleton, op. cit., p. 7.

p. 159 *It could accurately record business . . .* Carruthers and Espeland, op. cit., p. 48.

CHAPTER 7

p. 161 *his six-volume work on capitalism* . . .   Sombart's book has never been translated into English and his work has been neglected, largely because of his anti-Semitism and pro-Nazi position in 1930s Germany.

p. 162 'It is simply impossible . . .'   Sombart in Braudel, op. cit., p. 573.

p. 162 'one may indeed doubt . . .'   Sombart in Yamey, *Art and Accounting*, op. cit., p. 67.

p. 162 'a particular economic system . . .'   Garry D. Carnegie and Peter W. Wolnizer, *Accounting History Newsletter 1980–1989 and Accounting History 1989–1994*, Garland Publishing Inc., New York, 1996, p. 3.

p. 163 *French sociologist Eve Chiapello* . . .   The discussion of Marx and Sombart is mostly drawn from Eve Chiapello, 'Accounting and the birth of the notion of capitalism', *Critical Perspectives on Accounting*, vol. 18, issue 3, 2007, pp. 263–96.

p. 166 'Without looking too closely . . .'   Sombart in Braudel, op. cit., p. 573.

p. 168 'It was the perfection of accounting . . .'   Michael Olmert, *The Smithsonian Book of Books*, Smithsonian Books, Washington DC, 1992.

p. 168 *Although he does not go* . . .   Edwards and Walker, op. cit., p. 345.

p. 169 'The most general presupposition . . .'   Weber in Carruthers and Espeland, op. cit., p. 32.

p. 169 'a rational capitalistic establishment . . .'   Weber in Michael J. Fischer, 'Luca Pacioli on business profits', *Journal of Business Ethics*, vol. 25, no. 4, June 2000, pp. 299–312.

p. 169 'exalting the monetary unit . . .'   Joseph Schumpeter, *Capitalism, Socialism and Democracy*, Taylor & Francis e-Library, 1942, p. 123.

p. 170 'generates a formal spirit of critique . . .'   D. Stephen Long, *Divine Economy*, Routledge, London, 2000, p. 18.

p. 171 'Perhaps it is sufficient to ...' Yamey, *Art and Accounting*, op. cit., p. 82.

p. 172 'If [the merchant] be fortunate ...' Carruthers and Espeland, op. cit., p. 55.

p. 173 *In a 2000 essay on biomedical ethics* ... John H. Evans, 'Max Weber Meet the *Belmont Report*: Towards a sociological interpretation of principlism', in *Belmont Revisited: Ethical principles for research within human subjects*, James F. Childress, Eric M. Meslin and Harold T. Shapiro (eds), Georgetown University Press, Washington DC, 2005, p. 254.

CHAPTER 8

p. 177 'a presidential barrage of ideas ...' Robert Skidelsky, *John Maynard Keynes, 1883–1946: Economist, Philosopher, Statesman*, Pan Books, London, 2003, p. 506. All subsequent quotes from Keynes are from Skidelsky.

p. 179 *Keynes's framework introduced* ... Dale W. Jorgenson, J. Steven Landefeld and William D. Nordhaus (eds), *A New Architecture for the US National Accounts*, The University of Chicago Press, Chicago, 2006, p. 114.

p. 180 'survey and analyse an ...' Richard Stone, 'The Accounts of Society', Nobel Prize for Economics acceptance speech, 1984, http://nobelprize.org/nobel_prizes/economics/laureates/1984.

p. 180 'If you want to know why GDP ...' Nordhaus in Jon Gertner, 'The rise and fall of the GDP', *New York Times*, 10 May 2010.

p. 181 *Despite the concerns of Kuznets* ... J. Steven Landefeld, Eugene P. Seskin and Barbara M. Fraumeni, 'Taking the pulse of the economy: Measuring the GDP', *Journal of Economic Perspectives*, vol. 22, no. 2, Spring 2008, pp. 193–216, p. 195.

p. 183 *It was for this landmark 1940* ... Edwards and Walker, op. cit., p. 358.

p. 184 'Our estimates consisted of three . . .' Stone, op. cit.

p. 186 'national income measurement is . . .' Edwards and Walker, op. cit., p. 355.

p. 186 'only by a higher degree of aggregation . . .' Ibid.

p. 189 'by providing a consistent picture . . .' Jorgenson et al., op. cit., p. 114.

p. 189 *The SNA was revised again in 1993* . . . Edwards and Walker, op. cit., p. 358.

p. 191 'The quality of business decisions . . .' Survey of Current Business, January 2000.

CHAPTER 9

p. 194 *Sales had soared from US$2.3 billion* . . . Anna Pha, 'Enron: Capitalism in a nutshell', *Guardian*, 20 February 2002, p. 1. The discussion of Enron draws on Ann Pha's *Guardian* article and Niall Ferguson's *The Ascent of Money: A financial history of the world*, Penguin Books, Melbourne, 2008.

p. 198 'The experience of reading . . .' John Lanchester, *I.O.U.: Why everyone owes everyone and no one can pay*, Simon & Schuster, New York, 2010, p. 34.

p. 198 'models of clarity and translucency . . .' Ibid.

p. 200 'Given that modern corporations are . . .' Howard Ross, *The Elusive Art of Accounting: A brash commentary on financial statements*, The Ronald Press Company, New York, 1966, p. 5.

p. 201 'is responsible for accounting systems . . .' Edwards and Walker, op. cit., p. 417.

p. 201 *After its founder Ivar Kreuger* . . . Ibid., p. 419.

p. 203 'The impact of the Securities and Exchange . . .' Ibid., p. 209.

p. 205 *The design innovations of annual* . . . Ibid., p. 354.

p. 205 *Accounting's forward-looking postwar exuberance* . . . Ibid., p. 527.

p. 206 *These bodies increasingly* . . . Ibid., p. 163.

p. 207 *In 1991, the Bank of Credit and Commerce International* . . . Ibid., p. 422.

p. 207 *The fortunes of corporate Australia* . . . Ibid.. p. 420.

p. 208 *In 2003 the HIH Royal Commission* . . . Ibid., p. 409.

p. 209 *ABC Learning had a new auditor* . . . Colin Kruger, 'Lessons to be learnt from ABC Learning's collapse', *Sydney Morning Herald*, 2 January 2009. This discussion of ABC Learning is drawn largely from this article.

p. 212 'the straw that broke the corporate camel's . . .' Edwards and Walker, op. cit., p. 409.

p. 214 *Australia committed to the international* . . . Ibid., p. 411.

p. 215 'There is a certain circularity . . .' Volcker, quoted in Louis Uchitelle, 'Get tough, and stay tough, on big players', *Sydney Morning Herald*, 12 July 2010.

p. 216 'weak link in this chain' Jenkins, op. cit.

p. 217 'we will see more . . .' Ibid.

p. 218 'how Harold of Salisbury borrowed money . . .' Carruthers and Espeland, op. cit., p. 57.

p. 219 'accounts are used to . . .' Ibid., p. 47.

p. 220 'Most are idiot savants brought . . .' Frank Ahrens, 'For Wall Street's math brains, miscalculations', *Washington Post*, 21 August 2007.

p. 220 'Math's universal principles . . .' Ibid.

p. 221 'Every time a top party official said something . . .' Naomi Klein, *The Shock Doctrine*, Penguin Books, Camberwell, 2007, p. 207.

p. 222 *Economist Raj Patel points out that* . . . The discussion of the corporation draws extensively on Raj Patel, *The Value of Nothing*, Black Inc., Melbourne, 2009, p. 41.

p. 222 *Enron is revealed as having behaved* . . . Niall Ferguson, *The Ascent of Money: A financial history of the world*, Penguin Books, Melbourne, 2008, p. 172.

p. 225 'There has been much hullabaloo . . .' *The Economist*, 9 February 2006, p. 16.

CHAPTER 10

p. 228 *So sacred is the single GDP* . . . Gertner, op. cit.

p. 230 'its pollution-free environment . . .' 'Valuing the Environment: Measuring social welfare', University of Wollongong, www.uow. edu.au/~sharonb/STS300/valuing/measuring/national.html.

p. 230 'The national accounts are a macroeconomic . . .' www.abs. gov.au/ausstats/abs@.nsf/Previousproducts/5206.0Feature%20 Article80Sep%202002?opendocument&tabname=Summary&pro dno=5206.0&issue=Sep%202002&num=&view=.

p. 231 'as so many economists . . .' 'The time is ripe for green account-ing', European Environment Agency, 23 September 2009, www. eea.europa.eu/articles/the-time-is-ripe-for-green-accounting.

p. 232 *Following the 2004 Boxing Day tsunami* . . . Klein, op. cit., p. 391.

p. 235 'Congress made thinking . . .' 'GPI—GDP is killing us', Linda Baker, 31 May 2010, http://tangibleinfo.blogspot.com/2010/05/ gpi-gdp-is-killing-us.html.

p. 237 'Honeybee pollination activity . . .' Ibid.

p. 237 'nature's services are not, in fact . . .' Ibid.

p. 237 'poverty will only be made history . . .' Partha Dasgupta, 'The welfare economic theory of green national accounts', *Environmen-tal and Resource Economics*, vol. 42, 2009, January, pp. 3–38, p. 8.

p. 238 'On the basis of traditional measures . . .' Ibid., p. 9.

p. 238 'By continually depleting and damaging . . .' 'Valuing the Environment', op. cit.

p. 240 *The carbon storage, or sequestration* . . . ' "Natural account-ing" essential for poverty reduction', United Nations Environment Programme, 12 October 2005, www.unep.org/Documents.Multi-lingual/Default.asp?DocumentID=455&ArticleID=4998&l=en.

p. 241 *A 2003 project in New York City* . . . Corey Kilgannon, 'Get that oak an accountant', *New York Times*, 12 May 2003.

p. 242 'the possibility of financial recession . . .' Juliette Jowit, 'World is facing a natural resources crisis worse than financial crunch', *Guardian*, 29 October 2008.

p. 243 'is told to maximize GDP . . .'   'Time is ripe for green accounting', op. cit.

p. 243 'the economic measure itself . . .'   Ibid.

p. 244 'the inclusion of more non-market . . .'   Paul Ormerod, *The
Death of Economics*, Faber & Faber, London, 1994, p. 57.

p. 244 'a heightened focus on environmental indicators . . .'   Gertner,
op. cit.

p. 245 'I told Mahbub . . .'   Ibid.

p. 246 'an artefact . . .'   Ibid.

p. 247 *It involves working out . . .*   'Time is ripe for green accounting',
op. cit.

p. 247 'The message is clear . . .'   Ibid.

p. 248 *Corporations must be strictly . . .*   Juliette Jowit, 'UN biodiversity report calls for global action to prevent destruction of nature',
Guardian, 21 May 2010.

Epilogue

p. 250 *This is the cost-benefit analysis . . .*   Lewis Hyde, *The Gift: Creativity and the artist in the modern world*, Random House, New York,
2007, p. 81.

p. 252 'In practical terms . . .'   Crosby, op. cit., p. 229.

p. 253 'What we measure affects what we do . . .'   Gertner, op. cit.

p. 253 'there are few . . .'   Richard K. Fleischman, Vaughan S. Radcliffe
and Paul A. Shoemaker (eds), *Doing Accounting History: Contributions to the development of accounting thought*, Elsevier Science Ltd,
Oxford, 2003, p. 3.

BIBLIOGRAPHY

BOOKS

Aho, James, *Confession and Bookkeeping: The religious, moral and rhetorical roots of modern accounting*, State University of New York Press, Albany, 2005.

Alberti, Leon Battista, *On Painting*, trans. John R. Spencer, Routledge & Kegan Paul, London, 1967.

Allen, Christopher, *Jeffrey Smart, Unpublished Paintings 1940–2007*, Australian Galleries, Collingwood, 2008.

Angelini, Alessandro, *Piero della Francesca*, Scala, Florence, 1985.

Art Gallery of New South Wales, *The Moderns*, Art Gallery of New South Wales Catalogue, Sydney, 1984.

Atalay, Bulent, *Math and the Mona Lisa: The art and science of Leonardo da Vinci*, Smithsonian Books, New York, 2006.

Banker, James R., *The Culture of San Sepolcro during the Youth of Piero della Francesca*, University of Michigan Press, Ann Arbor, 2003.

Bertelli, Carlo, *Piero della Francesca*, trans. Edward Farrelly, Yale University Press, New Haven, 1992.

Braudel, Fernand, *Civilization and Capitalism, 15th–18th Century*, William Collins Sons & Co. Ltd, London, 1982.

Brown, R. Gene and Kenneth S. Johnston (eds), *Paciolo on Accounting*, McGraw-Hill Book Company Inc., New York, 1963.

Brown, Richard, *A History of Accounting and Accountants*, T.C. & E.C. Jack, Edinburgh, 1905.

Buchan, James, *Frozen Desire: An enquiry into the meaning of money*, Picador, London, 1998.

271

Carboni, Stefano, *Venice and the Islamic World 828–1797*, Metropolitan Museum of Art, Yale University Press, New York, 2007.

Carnegie, Garry D. and Peter W. Wolnizer, *Accounting History Newsletter 1980–1989 and Accounting History 1989–1994*, Garland Publishing Inc., New York, 1996.

Chatfield, Michael, *A History of Accounting Thought*, Krieger Publishing Co., Florida, 1977.

Childress, James F., Eric M. Meslin and Harold T. Shapiro (eds), *Belmont Revisited: Ethical principles for research with human subjects*, Georgetown University Press, Washington, 2005.

Clark, Kenneth, *Landscape into Art*, John Murray Ltd, London, 1949.

——*Piero della Francesca*, Phaidon, Oxford, 1969.

Crosby, Alfred W., *The Measure of Reality: Quantification and western society, 1250–1600*, Cambridge University Press, Cambridge, 1997.

Davies, Norman, *Europe: A history*, Pimlico, London, 1997.

Defoe, Daniel, *Robinson Crusoe*, Penguin, Harmondsworth, 1985.

——*The Complete English Tradesman*, 1725–27, www.online-literature.com/defoe/english-tradesman.

Dell'Arco, Maurizio Fagiolo, *Piero della Francesca e il Novecento*, catalogue of the 1991 Piero della Francesca exhibition in Sansepolcro.

Edgerton, Samuel Y., *The Mirror, the Window and the Telescope: How Renaissance linear perspective changed our vision of the universe*, Cornell University Press, New York, 2009.

Edwards, John Richard and Stephen P. Walker (eds), *The Routledge Companion to Accounting History*, Routledge, Abingdon, Oxon, 2009.

Eisenstein, Elizabeth L., *The Printing Press as an Agent of Change*, Cambridge University Press, Cambridge, 1979.

——*The Printing Revolution in Early Modern Europe*, Cambridge University Press, Cambridge, 1983.

Emmer, Michele, *Matematica e cultura 2003*, Springer-Verlag Italia, Milan, 2003.

Erasmus, Desiderius, *In Praise of Folly*, Reeves and Turner, London, 1876.

Fauvel, John and Jeremy Gray (eds), *The History of Mathematics: A reader*, MacMillan Press, London, 1990.

Ferguson, Niall, *The Ascent of Money: A financial history of the world*, Penguin Books, Melbourne, 2008.

Fibonacci, *Liber abaci*, Springer Publishing, New York, 2002.

Field, J.V., *Piero della Francesca: A mathematician's art*, Yale University Press, New Haven, 2005.

Fleischman, Richard K., Vaughan S. Radcliffe and Paul A. Shoemaker (eds), *Doing Accounting History: Contributions to the development of accounting thought*, Elsevier Science Ltd, Oxford, 2003.

Geijsbeek, John B., *Ancient Double-Entry Bookkeeping: Luca Pacioli's treatise*, 1914, reprinted by Nihon Shoseki Ltd, Osaka, 1975.

Gillispie, Charles Coulston (ed.), *Dictionary of Scientific Biography*, Charles Scribner's Sons, New York, 1974.

Giusti, Enrico, *Luca Pacioli et la Matematica del Rinascimento*, Petruzzi Editore, Citta di Castello, 1998.

Goethe, Johann Wolfgang von, *Wilhelm Meister's Apprenticeship*, Bell & Daldy, London, 1867.

Grendler, Paul F., *The Universities of the Italian Renaissance*, Johns Hopkins University Press, Baltimore, 2002.

——*Renaissance Education Between Religion and Politics*, Ashgate Publishing, Farnham, 2006.

Hockney, David, *Secret Knowledge: Rediscovering the lost techniques of the Old Masters*, Thames & Hudson, London, 2001.

Huizinga, Johan, *Erasmus and the Age of Reformation*, Dover Publications, Mineola, 2001.

Hyde, Lewis, *The Gift: Creativity and the artist in the modern world*, Random House, New York, 2007.

Jardine, Lisa, *Worldly Goods*, Macmillan, London, 1996.

Jorgenson, Dale W., J. Steven Landefeld and William D. Nordhaus (eds), *A New Architecture for the US National Accounts*, The University of Chicago Press, Chicago, 2006.

Kemp, Martin, *Leonardo*, Oxford University Press, Oxford, 2004.

Klein, Naomi, *The Shock Doctrine*, Penguin Books, Camberwell, 2007.

Lanchester, John, *I.O.U.: Why everyone owes everyone and no one can pay*, Simon & Schuster, New York, 2010.

Lane, Frederic C. and Reinhold C. Mueller, *Money and Banking in Medieval and Renaissance Venice*, The Johns Hopkins University Press, Baltimore, 1985.

Langan, Celeste, *Romantic Vagrancy: Wordsworth and the simulation of freedom*, Cambridge University Press, Cambridge, 1995.

Littleton, A.C., *Accounting Evolution to 1900*, Russell & Russell, New York, 1966.

Livio, Mario, *The Golden Ratio*, Broadway Books, New York, 2002.

Long, D. Stephen, *Divine Economy*, Routledge, London, 2000.

Lyons, Jonathan, *The House of Wisdom: How the Arabs transformed western civilization*, Bloomsbury, London, 2009.

Machiavelli, Niccolò, *The Historical, Political and Diplomatic Writings*, J.R. Osgood & Co., Boston, 1882.

McCraw, Thomas K. (ed.), *Creating Modern Capitalism: How entrepreneurs, companies, and countries triumphed in three industrial revolutions*, Harvard University Press, Harvard, 1995.

Marani, Pietro C., Roberto Cecchi and Germano Mulazzini, *Il Cenacolo*, Electa, Milan, 2008.

Morris, Jan, *Venice*, Faber & Faber, London, 1993.

Nicholl, Charles, *Leonardo da Vinci: The flights of the mind*, Penguin, London, 2004.

Nobes, Christopher W. (ed.), *The Development of Double Entry: Selected essays*, Garland Publishing Inc., New York, 1984.

Oelker, Maria, *Sansepolcro, A City Guide*, Colori di Toscana Editore, Florence, 2008.

Olmert, Michael, *The Smithsonian Book of Books*, Smithsonian Books, Washington DC, 1992.

Origo, Iris, *The Merchant of Prato: Francesco di Marco Datini*, Jonathan Cape, London, 1957.

Ormerod, Paul, *The Death of Economics*, Faber & Faber, London, 1994.

Pacioli, Luca, *Summa de arithmetica, geometria, proportione et proportionalità*, Paganino de Paganini, Venice, 1494.

Parker, R.H. and B.S. Yamey, *Accounting History: Some British contributions*, Clarendon Press, New York, Oxford, 1994.

Parks, Tim, *Medici Money: Banking, metaphysics and art in fifteenth-century Florence*, Profile Books, London, 2006.

Patel, Raj, *The Value of Nothing*, Black Inc., Melbourne, 2009.

Poovey, Mary, *A History of the Modern Fact: Problems of knowledge in the sciences of wealth and society*, University of Chicago Press, Chicago, 1998.

Pounds, N.J.G., *An Economic History of Medieval Europe*, Longman, New York, 1994.

Reilly, Robin, *Josiah Wedgwood*, Thames & Hudson, London, 1994.

Repetto, Robert, William Magrath, Michael Wells, Christine Beer and Fabrizio Rossini, *Wasting Assets: Natural resources in the national income accounts*, World Resources Institute, Washington, 1989.

Richardson, B., *Printing, Writers and Readers in Renaissance Italy*, Cambridge University Press, Cambridge, 1999.

Rose, Paul Lawrence, *The Italian Renaissance of Mathematics: Studies on humanists and mathematicians from Petrarch to Galileo*, Librarie Droz, Geneva, 1975.

Ross, Howard, *The Elusive Art of Accounting: A brash commentary on financial statements*, The Ronald Press Company, New York, 1966.

Rouse Ball, W.W., *A Short Account of the History of Mathematics*, Dover Publications Inc., New York, 1960.

Rowland, Ingrid D., *The Culture of the Italian Renaissance: Ancients and moderns in sixteenth-century Rome*, Cambridge University Press, Cambridge, 1998.

Russell, Bertrand, *A History of Western Philosophy*, Unwin Paperbacks, London, 1984.

Rylands, Philip, *Peggy Guggenheim Collection*, Guggenheim Museum Publications, New York, 2007.

Schumpeter, Joseph, *Capitalism, Socialism and Democracy*, 1942, Taylor & Francis e-Library.

Seife, Charles, *Zero: The biography of a dangerous idea*, Penguin, New York, 2000.

Severini, Gino, *The Life of a Painter*, trans. Jennifer Franchina, Princeton University Press, Princeton, 1995.

Simpson, J.A. and E.S.C. Weiner, *The Oxford English Dictionary*, second edition, Clarendon Press, Oxford, 1989.

Skidelsky, Robert, *John Maynard Keynes, 1883–1946: Economist, philosopher, statesman*, Pan Books, London, 2003.

Skira Guide, *The Castello Sforzesco of Milan*, Skira Guide, Milan, 2008.

Spengler, Oswald, *Decline of the West*, Oxford University Press, New York, 1991.

Swetz, Frank J., *Capitalism and Arithmetic: The new math of the fifteenth century*, Open Court, La Salle, 1987.

Taylor, R. Emmett, *No Royal Road: Luca Pacioli and his times*, Arno Press, New York, 1980.

Tolstoy, Leo, *Anna Karenina*, Penguin Books, London, 2006.

Vasari, Giorgio, *The Lives of the Artists*, Oxford University Press, New York, 1998.

Veltman, Kim H., in collaboration with Kenneth D. Keele, *Studies on Leonardo da Vinci I: Linear perspective and the visual dimensions of science and art*, Deutscher Kunstverlag, Munich, 1986.

Watkins, Renée, *The Family in Renaissance Florence*, University of South Carolina Press, Columbia, 1969.

Wood, Jeryldene M. (ed.), *The Cambridge Companion to Piero della Francesca*, Cambridge University Press, Cambridge, 2002.

Yamey, Basil S., *Art and Accounting*, Yale University Press, New Haven, 1989.

——*Essays on the History of Accounting*, Arno Press, New York, 1978.

Zilsel, Edgar, *The Social Origins of Modern Science*, Kluwer Academic Publishers, Dordrecht, 2003.

Journals

Achenbach, Joel, 'All the president's pennies: Washington, the meticulous businessman', *Sydney Morning Herald*, 17–18 October 2009.

Ahrens, Frank, 'For Wall Street's math brains, miscalculations', *Washington Post*, 21 August 2007.

Bushaw, Donald W., 'Rediscovering the Archimedean Polyhedra: Piero della Francesca, Luca Pacioli, Leonardo da Vinci, Albrecht Dürer, Daniele Barbaro and Johannes Kepler', *The College of Mathematicians Journal*, Washington, vol. 29, issue 2, March 1998, pp. 176–88.

Calhoun, Ada, 'Count her in: Denise Schmandt-Besserat's new way of seeing', *The Austin Chronicle*, 10 December 1999.

Carruthers, Bruce G. and Wendy Nelson Espeland, 'Accounting for rationality: Double-entry bookkeeping and the rhetoric of economic rationality', *American Journal of Sociology*, vol. 97, no. 1, July 1991, pp. 31–69.

Chiapello, Eve, 'Accounting and the birth of the notion of capitalism', *Critical Perspectives on Accounting*, vol. 18, issue 3, 2007, pp. 263–96.

Economist, The, 'Not all on the same page', 1 July 2010.

Fischer, Michael J., 'Luca Pacioli on business profits', *Journal of Business Ethics*, vol. 25, no. 4, June 2000, pp. 299–312.

Gertner, Jon, 'The rise and fall of the GDP', *New York Times*, 10 May 2010.

Gittins, Ross, 'Why economists didn't see the big crunch coming', *Sydney Morning Herald*, 17 July 2010.

International Herald Tribune, 'Experts link Leonardo da Vinci to chess puzzles in long-lost Renaissance treatise', 14 March 2008.

Jowit, Juliette, 'UN biodiversity report calls for global action to prevent destruction of nature', *Guardian*, 21 May 2010.

——'World is facing a natural resources crisis worse than financial crunch', *Guardian*, 29 October 2008.

Keene, Raymond, 'Renaissance chess master and the Da Vinci decode mystery', *The Times* online, 10 March 2008.

Kilgannon, Corey, 'Get that oak an accountant', *New York Times*, 12 May 2003.

Kruger, Colin, 'Lessons to be learnt from ABC Learning's collapse', *Sydney Morning Herald*, 2 January 2009.

Lall Nigam, B.M., 'Bahi-Khata: The pre-Pacioli Indian double-entry system of bookkeeping', *Abacus*, vol. 22, no. 2, September 1986, pp. 148–61.

Lanchester, John, 'It's finished', *London Review of Books*, 28 May 2009.

Landefeld, J. Steven, Senate Commerce Committee Hearings on 'Rethinking GDP', 12 March 2008.

Landefeld, J. Steven, Eugene P. Seskin and Barbara M. Fraumeni, 'Taking the pulse of the economy: Measuring GDP', *Journal of Economic Perspectives*, vol. 22, no. 2, Spring 2008, pp. 193–216.

MacAskill, Ewen, 'Barack Obama's crackdown bill on Wall Street wins Senate backing', *Guardian*, 15 July 2010.

McDonald, Lucy, 'And that's renaissance magic', *Guardian*, 10 April 2007.

——'Now you see it: Forgotten magic manual contains original da Vinci code', *Sydney Morning Herald*, 20 April 2007.

Mackinnon, Nick, 'The portrait of Fra Luca Pacioli', *The Mathematical Gazette*, vol. 2, 1993, pp. 130–219.

McVeigh, Karen, 'Why golden ratio pleases the eye: US academic says he knows art secret', *Guardian*, 28 December 2009.

Martinelli, Alvaro, 'Notes on the origin of double-entry bookkeeping', *Abacus*, vol. 13, issue 1, 1977, pp. 3–27.

Mills, Geoffrey T., 'Early accounting in northern Italy: The role of commercial development and the printing press in the expansion of double-entry from Genoa, Florence and Venice', *Accounting Historians Journal*, vol. 21, June 1994, pp. 81–96.

Nobes, C., 'Were Islamic records precursors to accounting books based on the Italian method?', *Accounting Historians Journal*, vol. 28, no. 2, 2001, pp. 207–14.

Peragallo, Edward, 'The ledger of Jachomo Badoer: Constantinople September 2, 1436 to February 26, 1440', *The Accounting Review*, vol. 52, no. 4, October 1977, pp. 881–92.

Pha, Anna, 'Enron: Capitalism in a nutshell', *Guardian*, 20 February 2002.

Rabinowitz, Allan M., 'Who was Luca Pacioli?', *The CPA Journal*, vol. 79, no. 2, 1 February 2009, pp. 16–19.

Richardson, Alan J., 'Strategies in the development of accounting history as an academic discipline', *Accounting History*, vol. 13, no. 3, August 2008, pp. 247–80.

Sangster, A., G.N. Stoner and P. McCarthy, 'The market for Luca Pacioli's *Summa Arithmetica*', *The Accounting Historians Journal*, vol. 35, June 2008, pp. 111–34.

Schmandt-Besserat, Denise, 'Signs of life', *Odyssey*, January/February 2002, pp. 6, 7 and 63.

——'One, two ... three', *Odyssey*, September/October 2002, pp. 6–7.

Uchitelle, Louis, 'Get tough, and stay tough, on big players', *Sydney Morning Herald*, 12 July 2010.

Watts, Jonathan, 'Are accountants the last hope for the world's ecosystems?', *Guardian*, 28 October 2010.

Weis, William L., 'Luca Pacioli: Renaissance accountant', *Journal of Accounting*, 1 November 1991, pp. 51–4.

Williams, John J., 'A new perspective on the evolution of double-entry bookkeeping', *The Accounting Historians Journal*, vol. 5, Spring 1978, pp. 29–39.

Yamey, B.S., 'The historical significance of double-entry bookkeeping: Some non-Sombartian claims', *Accounting, Business and Financial History*, vol. 15, issue 1, March 2005, pp. 77–88.

Zaid, O.A., 'Were Islamic records precursors to accounting books based on the Italian method?', *Accounting Historians Journal*, vol. 27, no. 1, pp. 73–90.

ONLINE SOURCES

AccountAble, issue 6: October–December 2005, http://uttardayee. freewebspace.com/Accountable_Asia.

Art: Bookkeeping, Double-entry Bookkeeping in Medieval Italy, www. franzarlinghaus.de/Bookkeeping.html.

Baker, Linda, 'GPI—GDP is killing us', 31 May 2010, http://tangibleinfo. blogspot.com/2010/05/gpi-gdp-is-killing-us.html.

Batuman, Elif, 'The windmill and the giant: Double-entry bookkeeping in the novel', www.elifbatuman.net/the-windmill-and-the-giant-summary.

Birkin, Frank, 'Leaders challenge "business as usual"', accessed July 2009, www.shef.ac.uk/management/staff/profile/birkin.html.

Carolingian Polyptyques, www.le.ac.uk/hi/polyptyques/capitulare/ latin2english.html.

Concise Encyclopedia of Economics, The, Simon Kuznets (1901–1985), 2008, www.econlib.org/library/Enc/bios/Kuznets.html.

Costa, Massimo and Patrizia Torrecchia, 'Value and accounting between history and theory, the Italian case', 2008, www.cardiff. ac.uk/carbs/conferences/abfh2008/costa.pdf.

Dasgupta, Partha, 'The welfare economic theory of green national accounts', 2008, www.econ.cam.ac.uk/faculty/dasgupta/ 08/10640_2008_9223_OnlinePDF.pdf.

DragonBear, www.dragonbear.com/champagne.html.

Durning, Alan, 'A new chance to fix GDP', 2008, www.worldchanging. com/archives/007896.html.

Eggermont, Christian, 'Christian Eggermont's disentanglement', accessed February 2009, www.win.tue.nl/~ceggermo/puzzels/ disentanglement.

Fondazione Istituto Internazionale di Storia Economica, 'F. Datini', www.institutodatini.it.

'GDP: One of the great inventions of the 20th century', *Survey of Current Business*, January 2000, www.bea.gov/scb/account_articles/general/ 0100od/maintext.htm.

Giroux, Gary, 'Accounting history page', 1999, http://acct.tamu.edu/giroux/history.html.

Heeffer, Albrecht, 'From problem solving to argumentation, Pacioli's appropriation of abbacus algebra', Centre for Logic and Philosophy of Science, Ghent University, accessed May 2009, http://logica.ugent.be/centrum/.

——'On the curious historical coincidence of algebra and double-entry bookkeeping', November 2009, http://logica.ugent.be/albrecht/thesis/FOTFS2008-Heeffer.pdf.

Huxley, Aldous, 'The best picture', 1925, www.paradoxplace.com/Perspectives/Italian%20Images/Montages/Art/Best%20Picture%20Huxley%20Essay.pdf.

Jenkins, Jolyon, 'A brief history of double-entry bookkeeping', BBC podcast, March 2010, www.bbc.co.uk/programmes/b00r402b.

Kuznets, Simon, Nobel Prize for Economics lecture, 1971, http://nobelprize.org/nobel_prizes/economics/laureates/1971/kuznets-lecture.html.

'"Natural accounting" essential for poverty reduction', 12 October 2005, www.portofentry.com/site/root/resources/feature_article/3417.html.

Sangster, Alan, 'Using accounting history and Luca Pacioli to teach double entry', Annual Accounting and Business History Research Unit Twentieth Annual Conference, 11–12 September 2008, www.cardiff.ac.uk/carbs/conferences/abfh2008/sangster2.pdf.

Stone, Richard, 'The accounts of society', Nobel Prize for Economics acceptance speech, 1984, http://nobelprize.org/nobel_prizes/economics/laureates/1984.

'Survey of Current Business', January 2000, www.highbeam.com/Survey+of+Current+Business/publications.aspx?date=200001.

'The time is ripe for green accounting', 23 September 2009, www.eea.europa.eu/articles/the-time-is-ripe-for-green-accounting.

'Valuing the Environment', University of Wollongong, 1996, www.uow.edu.au/arts/sts/sbeder/STS300/valuing/measuring/alternative.html.

Wentworth Group of Concerned Scientists, 'Accounting for nature: A model for building the national environmental accounts of Australia', May 2008, www.wentworthgroup.org.

White, Allen, 'The quiet revolution in business reporting', Ceres Publications, April 2007, www.vistaenergygroup.com/Download.html.

Williams, Rowan, 'Ethics, economics and global justice', text of a speech given on Saturday 7 March 2009 in Cardiff, from www.guardian.co.uk/world/2009/mar/09/rowan-williams-lecture-full-text.

Yamey, Basil S., 'Pacioli's *De Scripturis* in the context of the spread of double-entry bookkeeping', *Spanish Journal of Accounting History*, www.decomputis.org/dc/articulos_doctrinales/yamey.pdf.

INDEX